James Koppel Gutheim

The temple pulpit

a selection of sermons and addresses delivered on special occasions

James Koppel Gutheim

The temple pulpit
a selection of sermons and addresses delivered on special occasions

ISBN/EAN: 9783744745222

Printed in Europe, USA, Canada, Australia, Japan

Cover: Foto ©Lupo / pixelio.de

More available books at **www.hansebooks.com**

THE TEMPLE PULPIT

A SELECTION OF

SERMONS AND ADDRESSES

DELIVERED ON SPECIAL OCCASIONS

BY

REV. JAMES K. GUTHEIM,

MINISTER OF TEMPLE EMANU-EL, OF NEW YORK.

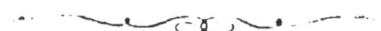

NEW YORK
JEWISH TIMES, 11 ANN STREET,

1872.

To
The Temple Emanu-El,
In
Affectionate Remembrance
Dedicated
By
The Author.

CONTENTS.

	PAGE.
I.—Address delivered at the Laying of the Corner-Stone of the Temple Emanu-El, New York, Oct. 31st, 1866	1
II.—Inaugural Sermon delivered at Temple Emanu-El, Nov. 14th, 1868. (First Part.)	13
III.—Inaugural Sermon delivered at Temple Emanu-El, Nov. 21st, 1868. (Second Part.)	22
IV.—Sermon delivered at the Consecration of the Temple Shaare Emeth, at St. Louis, Mo., Friday, August 27th, 1869	37
V.—Address delivered at the Laying of the Corner-Stone of Temple Sinai of New Orleans, Nov. 19th, 1871.	51
VI.—Sermon delivered at the Dedication of the Temple Ahawath Chesed of New York, Friday, April 19th, 1872	63
VII.—" The Spirit of God in Man," a series of our sermons delivered at Temple Emanu-El, Sabbath, March 2d, 1872. 1	77
VIII.—" The Spirit of God in Man." Sabbath, March 16th, 1872. 2	87
IX.—" The Spirit of God in Man." Sabbath, March 30th, 1872. 3	95
X.—" The Spirit of God in Man." Sabbath, April 13th, 1872. 4	105
XI.—Oration delivered at the Laying of the Corner Stone of the Home for Jewish Widows and Orphans of New Orleans	115

XII.—Oration delivered on the Fifth Anniversary of the Home for Jewish Widows and Orphans of New Orleans.................................... 129
XIII.—Address delivered at the Funeral of Judah Touro, at New Orleans, La., Jan. 20th, 1854............ 147
XIV.—Address delivered at the Funeral of Judah Tou.o, at Newort, R. I., June 7th, 1854............... 153
XV.—Address delivered at the Dedication of the Tomb of the Howard Association of New Orleans, and the Transfer of the Remains of its President, Victor Boullemet, April 15th, 1860................ . 159
XVI. - Address delivered at the Funeral of Joseph Fatman, at New York, Oct. 10th, 1869................... 165
XVII.—Opening Prayer delivered at the Semi-Centennial Anniversary of the Hebrew Benevolent and Orphan Asylum Society of New York, April 11th, 1872.... 171

I.

ADDRESS,

Delivered at the Laying of the Corner-Stone

OF THE

TEMPLE EMANU-EL,

Corner of Fifth Avenue and Forty-Third Street,

NEW YORK,

October 31st, 1866.

A sacred task has been performed. The corner-stone of a new house of worship is laid, and numbers have flocked together to witness this simple, though time honored ceremony, to testify by their presence the deep interest they feel in the erection of the projected edifice. Upon this foundation you have resolved to rear a house devoted to the worship of the Most High, the Creator and Governor of the Universe, the Father of all Mankind, the Guardian of Israel—a temple worthy of the name you bear and the religion you profess. With the completion of this edifice, you will possess a new religious home, wherein to assemble "from new moon to new moon, and from Sabbath to Sabbath," in order to pour out the inmost feelings of your hearts in prayer and in praise before the Omnipotent and all-kind Ruler of the Universe.

The corner-stone is deposited to a structure, which, at its completion, will be a noble monument of a pious enterprise, a bright ornament to our faith and to our people, and the just pride of its founders. Gradually this temple will rise, assume its grand proportions, and present to the eye of the admiring beholder the embodiment of the master's finished design, of the artist's noble conception. But not the material, however costly—nor the house, however beautiful—nor the decorations, however magnificent, will furnish cause for exultation. Architectural symmetry and ornamented walls are without significance, unless man invest them with his sentiments and feelings, his ideas and principles. The sentiments with which, at a future day, you will enter the portals of this temple will constitute its intrinsic ornament; the feelings which inspire our hearts at this hour render this day and this occasion holy, solemn and joyful.

Deep in the human soul the Creator has laid a foundation for the Divine. In the innermost recesses of the human heart He has treasured up the elements of the holy and heavenly, not in a dim, dreamlike, shadowy state, but illumined by a bright, self-conscious intelligence. They require not the helping hand of a skillful master to be moulded into form and expression. Spontaneously they burst forth, if not forcibly repressed, manifest their existence in the delight with which we contemplate every pious enterprise, the joy with which we regard every noble achievement, the sympathy which we exhibit with every sacred cause. Whatever is conceived in God, and for the honor of God, elevates and expands our heart; whatever is accomplished in God, and for the honor of God, fills our soul with a holy gladness. For a divine voice within us proclaims aloud קרבת אלהים טוב "The striving for the Divine is man's highest happiness."

The erection of a house of worship is coeval with the revelation of the law on Mount Sinai. The tabernacle of Moses in the wilderness was consructed at the special command of God, in the words, "And they shall make unto me a sanctuary and I will dwell among them," (Exod. xxv. 8.) This primitive, movable sanctuary was succeeded by the magnificent stationary temple at Jerusalem, and that again by the unpretending, widely scattered synagogues. For, although the glory of the Lord filleth the universe, although every spot where we call upon His name, He has promised us His blessing, yet in a house specially dedicated to His holy name we cannot fail to be imbued with the Divine, and to rise to a just appreciation of our duties as men, of our destiny as Israelites. I will dwell among you; that is, I will animate you with my spirit—the spirit of wisdom and understanding, the spirit of counsel and strength, the spirit of truth and love, the spirit of knowledge and the fear of God.

And this spirit is the spirit of our religion, the spirit of Judaism. Tabernacle and temple have vanished; but this spirit has survived. With our dispersion, it was wafted over the habitable globe, was enshrined in every synagogue. Neither the burning South, nor the frigid North; neither the rod of despotism, nor the shafts of persecution, nor the genial influence of liberty could weaken its force, abate our constancy, or shake our faith in the Holy One. We stand here as the connecting link of the past and future, anxious to transmit to posterity the sacred inheritance, the heavenly truths, the divine oracles received from our fathers, on the basis of which the temple of harmony and peace, of happiness and salvation for all mankind, shall one day be reared in its lofty grandeur.

The Jewish religion bears within itself the guarantee of its perpetuity. No incomprehensible mysteries constitute its groundwork. It is dependent upon no outward condition, coupled with no peculiar social or political relations, but is deeply and firmly rooted in the soil of eternal truth. No current of history can flood it away; no storm of events affect its existence; no progress of the human race supersede its importance, overshadow its growth, sap its foundation or impede its development. It addresses itself directly to the heart and mind of man, and must thrive and flourish, wherever the unsophisticated human heart manifests its warmth, and the unprejudiced human mind diffuses its light. From the time of Abraham, our father, to whom the Lord vouchsafed the promise, "that in his seed all the families of the earth shall be blessed;" from the day of the solemn proclamation on Sinai, " I am the Lord thy God," Israel has been the standard-bearer of the grand religious truth, which is destined, as we believe, to compass the ultimate redemption of the whole human race.

The Jewish religion is founded upon three cardinal principles that form its centre, and around which all the laws, commandments, ordinances and principles are revolving as the planets do around the sun. These are the doctrines of God, of man, and of the relations subsisting between God and man.

The first of these doctrines teaches and enjoins the belief in the absolute unity of God and his universal dominion and providence. In all the sacred records of the Bible, both historical, didactical and prophetical, this doctrine is inculcated in language so distinct and explicit as to admit of no other construction, The idea of a plurality in the godhead, of an exclusive national Deity, is foreign to our belief. At the very opening of Scripture, we are informed that God created the heavens, the unlimited space with its innumerable worlds, and the earth, upon which all men are moving and have their being. We are subsequently told that God made a covenant of peace and instituted the rainbow as the sign of this covenant, not only with mankind, but with all living creatures. Abraham worshipped God as the Creator of heaven and earth, as the righteous judge of the whole earth. Moses announced the Deity in that sublime sentence, which forms the essence and nucleus of our creed, "Hear, O Israel! the Lord is our God, the Lord is One!" And the lofty imagination of the psalmists and prophets was kindled and inspired by the great truth, "that the Lord is the God of the Universe," whose throne is the heaven, whose footstool the earth, whose rule and providence extend to all the sons of man, and whose name is praised from the rising of the sun to its setting

This cardinal principle, without which no true religion can be conceived, has been cherished throughout our chequered history. It is our peculiar mission to preserve it in its purity, to remain faithful to our trust, until to the God of the universe every knee shall bend in adoration, and every tongue shall swear fealty— "on that day the Lord will be One and His name One!"

The second doctrine concerning man is calculated to sow the seeds of charity and love in the heart of every true believer. It is embodied in the words of Scripture: "God created man in his own image." It constitutes the source from which spring and the goal towards which are tending, all the efforts for the amelioration of the human race. It is the basis of genuine humanity and philanthropy. It teaches us that love of man is founded on the grandeur of man's soul, its likeness to God, its immortality, its powers of endless progress; that, hence, it is our duty to look upon every man, to whatever nation he may belong, whatever creed he may profess, whatever language he may speak, as our brother. This doctrine finds its practical application in the divine commandment communicated through Moses. "Thou shalt love thy neighbor as thyself" (Lev. 19, 18). It is emphatically enforced in the beautiful words of the Prophet Malachi, (ii. 10), " Have we not all one Father ? Hath not one God created. us ? Why, then should we deal treachelously, one against the other, to profane the covenant of our Father ?" It impresses us with the conviction, that love and charity ought not to be confined to family, country or lineage ; that as our heavenly Father causes the sun to shine for the benefit of all, even so our religion teaches, that love and charity are universal blessings, and should knit all mankind in one sacred bond of brotherhood.

The third doctrine is conveyed in the Scriptural injunction, " You shall be holy, for I, the Lord your God, am holy," (Lev. 19, 2). This doctrine defines the relation of man to God, enjoins purity of thought and virtuous actions, and prohibits uncharitableness and enmity between man and man. For every wrong that we may perpetrate, every injury that we may inflict on our neighbor, every deed of violence that we may execute, every species of hatred and animosity that we may cherish in our bosom, every deception, fraud or falsehood, of which we may be guilty, in a word, every unholy thought, desire, word, or action in which we may indulge, alienates us from God, obscures and blurs the innate holiness and purity of our spiritual being.

These cardinal principles, of which I have given the merest outlines, constitute the life and soul of our religion, are incarnated in its every institution. Times may change ; new systems of government and sociology may rise in the horizon of history ; the human mind, in its laudable thirst for knowledge and improvement, may continue to dive into the arcana of nature, bring to light new and wonderful discoveries. cultivate the field of art and enlarge the empire of science ; development and progress in all that concerns mankind may remain the watchword of every age; yet these cardinal doctrines of our religion will remain truth, immovable truth, for-ever. They have stood the test of thousands of years, have passed triumphanthly through the various phases and ordeals of history, have been singularly active in the successively modified and progressive stages of civilization, and do this day, and ever will, assert their claim to universal recognition. But not by force, nor by violence, but by the spirit of of the Lord, will it be accomplished.

Judaism thus appears to us a castle looming forth above the ocean of time, standing as firm and unchanged as a granite promontory in the deep, amidst the waves and storms that beat upon it—its entrance supported by two imperishable columns; allegiance to God, the name of one; good will to man, the name of the other. It is the shining beacon enkindled by the Most High, when it pleased Him to make His will known to man. It is the code of peace, which teaches man to love his neighbor, to relieve the distressed, console the afflicted, succor the needy, assist even the enemy, when he is in need of our assistance. It is the true conception of the great Creator, recognizing in Him alone our Father, our God, our Ruler, our Savior.

These principles constitute the spiritual foundation upon which this temple will rise and be firmly planted. Whatever difference of opinion regarding other matters of faith and practice, of speculative and formal religion may exist, upon this solid basis every synagogue is established. There can be no dissent, no opposition from any quarter. These principles form the root and trunk of the sublime tree of our religion, which will find here a fruitful, genial soil. But whilst root and trunk have been and will be preserved in their pristine vigor and freshness, the branches and boughs, the luxuriant growth of many centuries have been carefully trimmed and fashioned, to afford an agreeable and wholesome shade to the present and future generations.

You stand here as the representatives of Reform—a position which you have occupied ever since the organization of your society. Your object, from its very inception, was, not to destroy, but to build up; not to weaken, but to strengthen the pillars of our faith. The great object of Reform, in my apprehension, is to maintain religion by promoting progress, by spreading an enlightened understanding of our religious tenets and institutions, by vindicating them from reproach and showing their claims to universal respect; by breathing into the young a generous devotion to them; to attract the luke-warm and indifferent by the beauty, appropriateness, solemnity and efficacy of our public worship. For the attainment of these great ends you have labored with an ardent zeal, unflinching determination and unswerving constancy; and it must afford you a holy satisfaction to contemplate this day the magnitude of your strength and influence, and the success that has crowned your efforts.

This corner-stone is an enduring testimony to the great results you have achieved. Next to the favor of Israel's God, to whose honor and glory you have offered your willing sacrifices in the prosecution of this holy work, your success is mainly owing to that harmony of sentiment and feeling, that concert of purpose and action which ever animated your ranks. The heaving agitation perceptible in many a congregation of Israel, arising from a struggle of old and new elements, of stability and progress, of the impossibility of getting repose by keeping things as they are; the jarring strife and dissension which divide many a Jewish congregation against itself, until the old and new have had time to adjust themselves to one another, or to merge their conflicting views, wishes and aspirations into a painfully devised compromise: this unhappy state of things is unknown to you. Peace and harmony constituted the banner under which you organized, under which you advanced; and, under this banner, you will continue to flourish and prosper.

But a short time will elapse when you will enjoy the reward of your sacrifices, the realization of your hopes, the fruition of your pious longings. In my mind's eye, I behold the sacred, noble pile raised aloft on this foundation in its beauty and grandeur—the temple erected in honor of the God of Israel, and dedicated to His holy name and service. Its portals are opened, and a pious throng are assembled within its walls. Pulpit, desk and choir combine to render the religious exercises solemn and edifying; to engage the heart and the mind of devout worshippers; to create the temple, what it is designed and destined to be, into a fountain of great and blessed influence. And as strangers from all parts will come hither and behold your fervent zeal, devout worship, your steady, intelligent piety, your warm openhearted benevolence, they will go from you as the ancient Israelite left the temple of Jerusalem, bearing with him impressions of God's majesty to the farthest part of his beloved land.

# II.

INAUGURAL SERMON

DELIVERED AT

TEMPLE EMANU-EL,

Sabbath, Nov. 14th, 1868.

FIRST PART.

"*Unto man belong the resolves of the heart, but from the Lord cometh the expression of the tongue.*" Prov. XVI. 1.

IT is with a feeling of deep anxiety that I appear before you this day—that I begin to speak. I stand here in response to your call. The resolves of my heart prompt me to speak; but will the expression of my tongue present to you a faithful picture of the sentiments and feelings that animate my soul in this hour? Will my voice be heard in this lofty, magnificent temple of the Lord? Will my words fall upon the *attentive* ears of this numerous congregation assembled before me? Will the sentiments I am about to utter touch a responsive chord in your hearts? Will my effort have a trace of that scholarly finish and logical acumen, which characterize the performances of my worthy colleague, the learned and justly revered rabbi of this congregation, with whom it will henceforth be my privilege to share this pulpit? In a word, shall I be able to realize, in a reasonable measure, the expectations based on my election to this responsible position?

I consult my heart, and its resolves give a cheering, encouraging reply. I look up prayerfully to my God; I put my firm trust in Him, whose kind providence has thus far guided and sustained my steps, that he may grant me the apposite expression of the tongue, so as to render my ministrations a blissful agency in the promotion of truth, light, and love. I lastly address myself to you, my beloved congregation, with the earnest entreaty and the firm hope, that my feeble voice be a welcome sound to your ears, and my words, coming from the heart, find a ready entrance into your hearts.

The office of minister is surrounded with many difficulties; it imposes a great responsibility. Impossible as it is in any situation of life, and more especially in any public position, to please everybody, it must nevertheless be the minister's duty to secure the approbation of the congregation, while at the same time no earthly consideration should induce him to swerve from the path of truth, or to act contrary to his conscience and inward conviction. Let us, then, in this hour of devotion inquire, "How can the religious teacher in Israel best promote the end of his mission; how he is to act in order that his labors may prove successful, and be deserving of the blessing of God?"

The answer is simple and comprehensive. Truth light, and love must be exemplified in his teachings and in his actions.

Truth is one of the most precious gifts, with which man was endowed by his Creator. Being a divine attribute, it assigns to him so exalted a position as to justify the words of the psalmist, "Thou hast made him a little less than angels!" Its transcendant quality has been best appreciated by our learned fathers, for they say "The seal of God is truth." Its influence on the mind has been well weighed, when they indited the beautiful admonition,

"Man should ever fear God in private, confess the truth, and speak truth in his heart." Why, then, should not all of us, why should not, in particular, the servant in the sanctuary of God live and act in truth ?

But what is truth, in this application of the term ? Truth is the correspondence of our thoughts and innermost convictions with our words and actions—a correspondence so precise and distinct, that not a diverging line should be perceptible to our mind. And it is only while thus living in truth that our labors will be truly blessed. Whoever can rise on the wings of the mind above the cloudy region of human error to the sunny heights of pure, untramelled thought, must certainly acknowledge, that truth alone imparts to man true dignity, as also heavenly bliss. But to be truthful, truthful in everything, truthful towards every one, is a problem the solution of which is attended with great difficulty. Thousands are prostrated by the trammels of superstition, the fetters of pride, the chains of ambition, the pressure of the passions, the mighty weight of gold. Truth alone is exalted above all degrading passions and human vanities ; truth alone reconciles all differences, surmounts all obstacles. Is it, then, saying too much, that the entire life of him must be truth, whose office and duty it is to expound and disseminate the law of truth, given by the God of truth ?

It is, therefore, an indispensable qualification of the preacher *to be a sincere friend of truth*. In whatever circumstances he may be placed, whatever the consequences resulting to him from his action, nothing must deter him from paying due homage to truth. No preconceived opinion, no prejudice, no self-love, no interest of any kind must bias his mind and sway his judgment. As a sincere friend of truth, he must strive with an ardent zeal to find it. The more conflicting the opinions on religious subjects have become in our day, the more calmly and deliberately must he search, in order to be able, correctly to distinguish between the true and the false. And this zeal must animate him so powerfully and completely, that it only ceases with the last breath he draws on earth. It is not enough for him to blindly accept whatever tradition has handed down, whatever custom has sanctioned, and to answer every query propounded to him by the authoritative, falacious dictum, " Whatever is, is right!" Far from it. His conviction must be the result of careful assiduous study. He must be able to trace effects to their legitimate causes, to separate the form from the substance, the essential from the incidental, the immutable from the temporal and local. If any one stands in need of a thorough, well-grounded, immovable conviction, it is undoubtedly the religious teacher, whose province it is to satisfy the inquirer and to convince the doubting and wavering. He cannot successfully teach the truth by hollow phrases; his words must be the mirror of his soul.

And in harmony with his teaching should be his life and actions. In the circle, in which he moves, his deportment must be open, candid, bearing the stamp of truth. While, on the one hand, he is often obliged, from the peculiar circumstances in which he may be placed, and for the sake of the cause in which he is engaged, to act with wise moderation, caution and prudence, he must never, on the other hand, from any motive whatsoever, so far forget himself as to stoop to base hypocrisy, and allow his actions to belie his inward conviction. In order to be trusted, he must be truthful in all the relations of life. No timidity, no fear, no prospect of reward must ever determine him to misrepresent truth by his words or actions. And should he even meet with opposition, should he even be misrepresented, calumniated and persecuted, he must not swerve from his purpose. The consciousness of having acted according to duty and conscience is ample reward. " Truth will conquer its way."

But how often do short-sighted mortals mistake error for truth, and pronounce firmness a visionary idea. Has not, for the last 1,800 years, our truthful religion been decried as an exploded system, and our faithful adherence to it been styled blinded stubborness? Well, then, we want some auxiliary to arrive at the clear truth. " Light shall prevail!" Can you conceive anything in nature more beneficial and grand than light? In our daily prayers we praise the Creator of light; every being joyfully greets the light; the first manifestation of the creative power of the Lord of the universe is—light. Who does not feel a holy sensation filling his bosom, whenever he reads the words in the first paragraph of Holy Writ: " There was light." The blessings of light are incalculable; they are divine. And here I do not merely speak of the material light that invests every visible object with form and outline; I refer more particularly to that spiritual light, which the Almighty has vouchsafed to bestow on those he created in his own image: namely, the light of reason and religion. " For the commandment is a lamp, and the law is light!" " The soul of man is a lamp of the Lord." Religion and reason combined form the spiritual light in man. It is true that he who never saw the light of day from his birth, or who was, by some misfortune, deprived of his sight at a later period, may, nevertheless, not altogether pass his days without joy or delight. But can he behold the splendor of the sun, the moon's silvery beams, the sparkling brilliancy of the stars? Does the azure sky, the mountain's grand scenery, the verdure of the forest, the meadow's variegated tints, the waving harvests of the field open to him an enchanting vista? Is he able to view the millions of charms so profusely displayed by nature and art? Can he look upon those who gave him birth and nursed and reared him, on the brother, the sister, and friend to whom he is warmly attached? Alas, no! Life's highest enjoyments, life's sweetest joys are denied him. And so, too, may he whose mental eye is overclouded and darkened by superstition and irreligion, who cannot see the sun of truth, not live altogether without joy or delight. But to appreciate properly and truly the mysterious workings of Providence, the destiny of man, the blissful emotions engendered by virtue, the invaluable blessing of Revelation, the humanizing effect of the faith in the absolute unity of God, and how refined and ennobled all mental culture is rendered, if joined to true religion, based on firm conviction—can he appreciate all this? Alas, no! These pure, spiritual enjoyments are utterly lost to him.

Well, then, it is the duty of the preacher in Israel to diffuse light, to impart clear information, and wherever the clouds of error and prejudice cover the mental vision to dispel them by the expression of his tongue. His teaching must be an emanation from, and in strict accordance with, the word of God. He is to fan the glimmering embers into a blaze, casting about a refulgent light. When Moses, the man of God, besought the Almighty "to let him see his glory;" when David, the pious king, sang "May the Lord let his countenance shine upon us"—when Solomon prayed that God might endow him with wisdom—what else did they desire but luminous knowledge? What else did all the God-inspired men, the prophets of old, endeavor to diffuse among the people, when they attacked the idolatry and superstition and denounced the mere form-and lip-service of their age, but the spread of luminous knowledge?

Such is the beautiful simplicity of our creed, that no blind belief is enjoined on the Israelite, but that he is commanded emphatically, to *know* the doctrines and principles of his faith, since to *know* is to *believe*. Those mystical incongruities and absurdities requiring implicit belief, which we meet elsewhere, are in no manner or way interwoven in our creed. " Thou shalt know the Lord thy God," is a commandment we find on almost every page of Scripture, where His existence and providence are adverted to. " Thou shalt meditate in the law, and teach it diligently to thy children," is enjoined with the like urgency. And if we examine the history of our fathers, of those times, especially, which are commonly denominated the dark ages, we shall find that, although the Israelite was shut out, as it were, from the light of the world, his obscure abode was illumined by the light of the Law. It was to him a source of consolation, of sweet enjoyment, while it kept alive in his bosom a hope of better days. If such was the practice of our fathers in adversity, shall we pursue an opposite course in our days of prosperity ? Is it not, on the contrary, our duty to obtain a clear knowledge of the essence and spirit of our holy religion, and be thus enabled to vindicate the purity and sublimity of its doctrines before the eyes of the world ? To awaken, therefore, and foster the spirit of inquiry, and a fervent yearning towards religious light, in the temple as well as in the school, is a sacred duty devolving upon the religious teacher.

Truth often produces a harsh effect. *Light* often leaves us cold. It is for this that mildness must be coupled with truth, that warmth was associated with the light. Both, therfore, will assert their beauty, efficiency and supremacy, if joined by *love*. Love is one of the cardinal principles of all true religion. It is the mighty link and tenure by which society is held together, the animating principle of the human heart. Before its salutary rays the differences of creed and opinion, the inequalities of fortune and position, vanish into air. The ties of family, friendship, connection, are woven and sustained under its heavenly influence. Love constitutes the very foundation of our religion, the living principle of the whole structure. Hence, the third requisite of the religious teacher is, that his words must breathe the spirit of love. It is true that, in the discharge of the duties of his calling, the preacher is often called upon to admonish and warn. But the expression of his tongue, although characterized by all the zeal and energy he is capable of, ought never to merge into seathing rebuke and denunciation. Whenever a son or daughter of Israel has fallen into sin, whenever in an unfortunate moment worldly considerations or passions gained the mastery, it is the duty of the religious teacher to recall the erring by mild admonition, wise moderation and gentle persuasion. "Love covereth all transgressions," is the beautiful maxim of the wise king. I would expatiate still more at length on the duties of the minister, and the relation he bears to his congregation, were it not that I intend to resume this subject on Sabbath next. Enough however, has been said to show that his calling is a difficult one, difficult on account of the momentous problem he is to solve—to do justice to his religion, to his conviction, to his God and his congregation. But he is sure to succeed, his labors are sure to be blessed, if he is actuated by truth, guided by light, prompted by love.

My friends, during the course of my ministerial career it has been my happy lot, to know something of the reciprocal affection which is calculated to steel our energies for renewed and vigorous efforts. My late sphere of action, far away in the sunny South, with all the cherished reminiscences of tokens of sincere love and tender solicitude extended to me and mine, is, at this solemn moment, fresh and vivid in my mind. The pain of recent separation has revealed the power of these affectionate ligaments, and memory shall never cease to recall the images of my dear friends left behind me, whose warm attachment and esteem I had secured, who, for a number of years, were my colaborers in the cause of religion, charity, and progress. To-day I have performed my first duty in your midst. If we are permitted to walk together as minister and congregation, need I assure you that your affection, your hearty esteem, will neither be unprized nor unreciprocated. Let me indulge the sweet hope, that I am addressing the members of a new congregation who, without exception, extend to me their right hand of welcome and fellowship. Next to the Divine approbation and that of my own conscience, I covet the sincere, intelligent, and just affection of my congregation. Without this my usefulness here will be a failure; with it, it will go on increasing till death or God's providence in other ways parts us. May, then, truth, light, and love characterize our intercourse, may our connection be based on mutual confidence and esteem, and it will redound to our salvation, to the consolidation of healthful progress and reform, to the glory of God and his everlasting covenant.

Almighty and most merciful God! Great is Thy name in the universe, and Thou art kind to all Thine creatures. From the distance Thou didst call me, from obscurity Thou didst lead me forth, that I might relate Thy wonders in this house dedicated to Thy holy name; that I might proclaim Thy will to those who seek Thee in truth. Grant me strength, O Father, to execute the mission on which I am sent, that I may not be ashamed through my errors, nor my congregation be ashamed through me. Guide and teach me, O God, and bless my ministration with Thy divine blessing. May error vanish and truth prevail! May the hearts of those, who are now exclusively bent on worldly objects, turn to Thee in sincerity and truth. May thy blessing rest on this congregation, so that prosperity, godliness and piety mark its onward career; may this temple prove a fountain of ever increasing truth, light and love. Guide us all in Thy goodness, for Thou art the God of our salvation, and in Thee we hope and trust. Amen.

III.

INAUGURAL SERMON

DELIVERED AT

TEMPLE EMANU-EL,

Sabbath, Nov. 21st, 1868.

SECOND PART.

*" He that reflecteth on a matter wisely
will find happiness; and whoso trusteth
in the Lord—happiness attend him."*
Pro. xvi 20.

EVERY relation of life has its peculiar duties ; every new engagement, which we contract, involves new obligations. The right to *demand* on the one hand implies the duty to *perform* on the other, and a clear knowledge of our respective rights and duties is a prerequisite to establish a good understanding and harmonius action. This rule holds good, whether we apply it to the general social compact or to special relations that are entered into by individuals or corporations.

In entering, therefore, on the duties of my office as English minister of this congregation, you will bear with me, if I endeavor to establish a clear understanding with regard to our relative positions, duties and expectations. The spirit of inquiry has penetrated every department of life, and the objects and ends of every profession and pursuit are weighed and scrutinized. The ministerial calling is not exempt from this scrutinity, nor does it claim such exemption. Its high purposes justify its existence. The interests it represents, it is true, are not comprised in the utilitarian tendency of the age; yet are these interests the most important and the most sacred within the range of human feelings, thoughts and aspirations. How dreary a solitude would life be without the light of revelation, without the consciousness of an ever-watchful Providence above us, without the hope of an endless hereafter! Through what a labyrinth of perplexities and contradictions touching his origin and destiny would man have to grope his way, if he do not possess a sure guide in the revealed Word of God! And in order to secure the blessings of our heaven-born religion to ourselves and posterity, congregations are formed, temples and synagogues erected, religious schools organized, teachers and ministers appointed. No Israelite, who has the interests of his religion at heart, can be indifferent to these institutions and appointments. He will promote the prosperity of the first and facilitate the efficiency of the latter. Hence the question will naturally arise, what are the relations subsisting between a congregation and its minister? What are the mutual expectations, which each party is justly entitled to cherish?

The relation subsisting between the minister and his congregation creates reciprocal obligations. The minister has his duties, most urgent, most important, unceasing. But while this is true on the one side, it is not less true on the other, that the congregation, by the election of a minister and the enjoyment of his services, bring themselves under corresponding responsibilities to him, to their religion and their God. Your election of a minister is on your part a purely voluntary act. But when it is *done*, while that relation subsists, while he continues faithful to his work, you cannot refuse to discharge the duties to which it gives rise, without guilt and dishonor. You will bear with me, then, to-day, if I should speak to you of some things, which have direct reference to myself and to my future ministry among you. Much as we anticipate from that attachment, so happily commenced between us, it will not prejudice our mutual confidence, it will facilitate our future intercourse, and lay a broader basis for harmonious action hereafter, if at the outset of our connection we understand each other and loock calmly and steadily at the duties, which we are bound reciprocally to perform.

In my last sermon I defined, in general terms, the course to be followed by the minister. He should be actuated by truth, guided by light, prompted by love. And it is necessary that his course should be thus truthful, clear and conciliatory, since the difficulties he is likely to encounter are of no ordinary character. Let us not disguise the fact, that with all the progress thus far achieved, things are yet in a state of transition, in the process of development. Although the congregation, in its aggregate capacity, is bound by the holiest ties—those of common lineage and religion,—and has united for a common object, that of worshipping the God of Israel according to the true spirit and intent of our holy religion; yet from the periodical accretion of new members, as well as from other obvious causes, it cannot fail, that some time must yet elapse, before the diversified opinions, habits, customs, predispositions, predilections of the individual members will be blended, so as to present a perfectly harmonious aspect in all matters appertaining to the worship and discipline of the temple and the religious practice in life. To persist in bringing about this happy consummation, to render the Temple the focus of religious light that is to radiate on every side, is the legitimate province of the minister.

On the other hand, it is a duty on the part of the congregation, in order to establish a perfect understanding, to cultivate an intimate acquaintance with the minister. They should seek and offer opportunities to know, as well as to become known to him. Mutual knowledge of of each other will lead to mutual esteem (if, indeed, such be at all deserving). Mutual knowledge, while it may reveal imperfections, will yet bring out into more striking light the predominant good feeling; it will enable him to adapt his instructions more perfectly to your character and understanding, and prepare you to listen with more profound attention to the truths he may utter. Do not look upon him as if he were a spy upon your conduct; as if his business were solely that of finding fault with your lives; as if he were a monk looking out of his sepulchral den with a green eye upon all the things you hold most dear. He is a man like yourselves; of the same social affections; the same intellectual perceptions of all that is beautiful in the world around us; of the same general infirmities incident to human nature. Do not treat him, therefore, with a distant respect, with the cold politeness of ceremony, as one whom you are to meet only on state occasions, but as one who is to be with you, a sympathizing friend in scenes of trial and of joy, the most thrilling and affecting this side of the grave.

The Jewish ministry does not constitute a peculiar order or privileged class of men. Its members have no other authority but that of the law, no power but that of truth, no influence but that of light and love. The time has happily passed, when obedience was enforced by anathema and excommunication. The bonds which now unite congregation and minister are: mutual confidence and esteem. And whenever these are wanting, the connection becomes irksome and fails in producing any good results.

As a congregation it is, further, your duty to be in prompt attendance at the stated times of divine service. This sanctuary—a speaking monument of your pious zeal and sacred munificence, an object of pride and glory to to the Jewish name—this sanctuary is to be *your* religious home as well as that of your minister. It would be disheartening indeed, if the devout attendants at the temple should consist of a small minority, while the principal part of the congregation were to keep aloof. Justly could he complain : " Why did I come when there is no man; why was I called, when there is none to answer ?" And when he comes forth, after days of mental toil, with his message addressed to you, it is neither honorable in you nor profitable for either, to find you absent. The idea of so much salary for so much labor, and when both parties have fulfilled that part of the contract, it is no farther matter, what course they pursue, is infinitely degrading to the mind that entertains it, while its influence disheartens and paralyzes the faithful servant of God. If, according to your expressed desire and solemn stipulation, your minister is bound to preach to you and to your children the word of God in the vernacular of the land; if the whole design, for which he has relinquished a field endeared to him by many tender and holy associations, was to gain a larger sphere of usefulness—then neither honor nor honesty, neither religion nor an elevated morality, can be satisfied with the mere payment of money on your part, while you do not come regularly to offer your worship to our Heavenly Father, and to hear the truth. Surely you have not agreed with me, to preach to empty benches. An automaton could effect that as well and better than a living man; for it has no nerves or affections to be lacerated and distressed by such an operation. There are reasons, indeed, which in God's sight will excuse absence from this sanctuary; but a little cold, a little rain, a little heat, or a little inconvenience produced by time or distance, will never justify the forsaking of the temple to any truly pious mind. Continue, therefore, I pray, the beautiful example I have witnessed these two Sabbaths. It is my hope that an honorable, just and elevated tone of feeling will, in this respect, ever characterize all the members of this congregation; that they will carry into practice the beautiful sentiment of the psalmist: "I rejoice, when they say to me, let us go into the house of the Lord!"

But your mere presence is not sufficient; it is your duty to give a reverential and careful attention to the services of God's house. The solemnity of your deportment should correspond with the sacredness of the place and of the worship here offered. The stranger, when he enters this place, should be impressed with awe—should be made irresistibly to feel, that he is among people, who know how to value the blessings of their revered, time-hallowed religion. Your children should grow up accustomed to your reverential and thoughtful conduct in the house of God. Never should they behold in you a light, supercilious air, or an indifferent, careless, perhaps sleepy countenance. You should offer the prayers of your heart with the true spirit of devotion; you should listen to the exposition of the word of God, not with a captious nor critical spirit, not with a desire for the mere drapery of the sermon, but with a healthful appetite for the truth. It should be your desire to hear *the truth*, rather than seek for the mere enjoyment of a gratified curiosity.

Nor is an attentive hearing sufficient. You will not do justice to your minister, if you do not compare his preaching with the word of God. No tradition, no assertion of the holiest minister that ever preached is to weigh a feather with you, unless it be in harmony with this revealed truth. My word is not to be your faith. You will do me great injustice, if you do not meditate and search for yourselves in the word of life. It is my prayer, that I may never utter one sentiment, never advance one opinion in this place, which the spirit of inspiration will not indorse. But be assured, whether I succeed in this or not, my efforts will be barren of their noblest results, if they fail in stimulating you to a careful and diligent study of the word of God, and the requirements of your religion. And while I thus urge you to an enlightened independence, I ought to warn you against that factious and criminal independence which finds fault with the preacher, either because he does not say all that you would like to have him say on all subjects, or because he may utter sentiments that cross the track of your opinions or your life. Of what worth to you is a man, who will not speak the *truth* on those subjects which are vital to your peace, your comfort, your salvation? Of what value to you is a man, whose cry is peace, peace, when you are in danger of eternal strife? What interest have you in hearing a man, who aims either to tickle your fancy, amuse your intellect, or sport about the mere flowers and drapery of this world, while he is afraid to analyze your character, unfold the great principles on which the noble structure of our heavenly religion is based, and urge you to tread the road of life! In the *truth* you have a fearful interest, but in error you have no interest. And hence the great question with you should ever be, Has the preacher uttered the truth? Is it in harmony, not with our preconceived opinions, but with the word of God? There are many of you proficient in secular pursuits, at whose feet I would willingly sit and receive instruction in those things, with reference to which your lives have been spent. But I should deem myself unworthy of my position here, unworthy of your confidence, if I were to permit any of you to dictate, what or how I shall preach, while I remain your minister. You have chosen me to fill this post, because you had confidence in me, that I would act wisely; that I would uphold and defend the banner of reform and progress, which you have so firmly planted; and it is my prayer, that God will strengthen me to meet, in this respect, your expectations and justify your confidence.

But my labors do not cease here, are not bounded by the walls of the temple; they extend farther. I refer here more particularly to the religious training of your children, in which sacred task it will be my duty to assist. If you are at all desirous of establishing your religion on a firm and enlightened basis, the religious education of the rising generation must not be neglected. They should early be taught the principles of our holy faith, and the beauty and sublimity of its doctrines be impressed on their minds; they should be early instructed in the language and history of their fathers, to recognize the ruling hand of Providence that shapes the destinies of nations; they should early be initiated into the practice of those high duties prescribed by our religion, "to do justice, to love kindness, and to walk humbly before the Lord," and when they become old, they will not depart therefrom. A solid, enlightened religious foundation should be laid in the minds of the young, so that when they grow up to become useful members of society, fitted for any pursuit they may choose to adopt, they may never cease to be good *Israelites* in the literal sense of the word, " champions in the cause of God!"

My friends, Providence has permitted me to enter on the duties of my office in your midst after nearly twenty-three years of ministerial labor in this country. Shifted to a new sphere of action, surrounded by new circumstances, I may have much to learn, you may have much to bear. Yet I trust, you will not find me an inapt scholar, while I anticipate on your part a kind disposition, that will not be eagle-eyed to detect infirmities, and a charity broad enough to cover many imperfections. To-day I renewedly devote myself wholly to your service, and to that of our holy religion. Whatever toil of mind or concern of heart appertains to this high position, whatever is just and right, *that* you are authorized to claim, nor will you find me backward in responding to it. And whatever a minister ought to ask of any congregation, whatever is just and right, and most for their highest good, he should ask of them, all that, you may be assured, will be expected of you. Being the first well-organized reformed congregation in this large and enterprising city, possessing a temple that rivals, if not surpasses, in beauty and magnificence, any Jewish house of worship in the world; living in the midst of an enlightened, liberal-minded community—you have a high and noble task to perform. Strange as it may sound, it is nevertheless true, that to the Gentile world Judaism is as yet only known by name, and all the interest evinced in its behalf proceeds more from a vague curiosity than a true appreciation of its merits. It is your duty, therefore, as well as your privilege, to continue the exercise of your efforts and of your influence for the spread of enlightened religious views, for the prosperity of our people and the accomplishment of its mission, for the triumph of truth, light and love, in this great Western World. You should take a noble pride in sustaining this congregation in all its arrangements, in its steady, intelligent piety, its warm, open-hearted benevolence, a model congregation—this temple, with its beautiful, solemn, elevating worship, a fountain of great and blessed influence. And as strangers from all parts come hither and behold your order, your growing numbers, your fervent zeal, your devout worship, your liberality, your ardent patriotism, they will go from us as the ancient Israelite left the temple, bearing with him impressions of God's majesty to the farthest parts of his beloved land.

IV.

SERMON

Delivered at the Consecration of the

TEMPLE SHAARE EMETH.

(GATES OF TRUTH.)

AT ST. LOUIS MO.

Friday, 27th of August 1869.

" This is the day, which the Lord hath appointed, we will rejoice and be glad thereon." Ps. cxviii. 24.

THIS invitation of the Psalmist to rejoicing and gladness finds a ready response in your hearts in this hour. For four long years have you anxiously looked forward to this day. From the moment that the ground was broken and active preparations were made for the erection of this sanctuary, the progress of the work was watched with anxious hopes and deep-felt solicitude, and from day to day you asked the question, מתי אבא ואראה פני אלהים " when may we enter this house and appear in the presence of God?" Your exertions and sacrifices are fully rewarded; your hopes and expectations fully realized. For the temple is now completed in all its beauty and magnificence; it stands here in its finished artistical symmetry, presenting that " silent harmony," with which architecture delights the eye of the beholder, and, " as a thing of beauty, will be a joy forever."

In uniting your efforts for this undertaking, you have nobly discharged a duty, which you owed to your religion and to your God—and whereas the faithful performance of duty imparts tranquility to the mind and awakens joyous sensations in the bosom, of what a pure and exalted nature must these emotions be, if such duty involve a holy purpose, if its discharge aim at the accomplishing of an object, that will redound to the benefit and salvation of ourselves and of those that will come after us. To realize an object so grand, to perpetuate the time-honored religion, which has been, for thousands of years, the light, the solace, the shield, the very life of Israel, you have entered on and accomplished this enterprise. With the dedication of this temple a new point of union is created for the scattered sons of Israel, a new sanctuary is established on freedom's soil, wherein to worship the God of our fathers, the God of heaven and earth, in conformity to His holy will, in accordance with our convictions. With hearts full of gratitude we have, therefore, "blessed the Lord our God, who has preserved us alive, sustained us in health, permitted us to enjoy this season," and to participate in the sacred rite of dedicating this house to His holy name.

In examining the history of the Jewish settlements in this country, the gradual formation of the congregations already established or yet in a state of incipiency, that are scattered over these States, it is a gratifying reflection, to observe the zeal and alacrity which ever were and still are manifested by our brethren: to rally round the standard of our religion, to unite in upholding the Divine creed revealed on Sinai and designated as the inheritance of the congregation of Jacob. This fact is the more gratifying, when the individual and sectional differences of those, who unite for religion's sake, are taken into consideration. Not a single case is known where a whole congregation in the Old World seized the wandering staff, to seek an asylum in the New World, as did the pilgrims of the Mayflower. Israelites immigrated as individuals or single families, spread over the country, until their number at a particular place warranted the formation of a religious body corporate. Nor had they anything more in common except their religion, but were, in most cases, in every other respect, strangers to each other. But there is something in the soul of the Israelite, which prompts him to join his brother-Israelite for the consolidation of the religious truths entrusted to him; and that is, the consciousness of the importance of his mission, for which he is selected: to be the bearer and guardian of divine truth for all times and to all nations.

The ceremony of dedication, which we this day celebrate with holy joy and grateful hearts towards our God and merciful Protector, is of deep importance to ourselves, of absorbing interest to the stranger. Simple and solemn in its conception, it is a type of the devotional exercises, that will henceforward take place within these walls. No imcomprehensible mystery is interwoven in our creed. The absolute unity of God, as erst proclaimed by Abraham and taught by Moses, yet forms the basis and the keystone of our belief. God is our father, and we are his children—man is created in the image of God and destined to immortality, are cardinal doctrines of our faith. "The Lord is the immutable, eternal Being, the omnipotent God, merciful and gracious, long-suffering and abundant in beneficence and truth, keeping mercy even unto the thousandth generation, forgiving iniquity, transgression and sin"—this heavenly message justifies our hope in salvation. The divine commandment, "Thou shalt love thy neighbor as thyself," is the immovable fountain-head of our moral law, and the invariable guide of our practice. These truths, that are within the grasp of the simplest understanding, and, as we are taught and firmly believe, will one day be universally acknowledged, form the spiritual basis of our temple. The spirit of these truths is embodied in every prayer we utter, in every religious discourse that is pronounced from a Jewish pulpit. Amidst all the transformations which, for thousands of years, have changed the face of the globe, amidst the downfall of thrones and the crash of empires, we have preserved the glorious legacy inherited from our fathers: of being the depositaries of the heaven-revealed word—of being the living witnesses of the living God, through all times and in all zones.

These considerations naturally suggest themselves on an occasion like this. The dedication of this temple bears testimony to the vital power of our religion, the sublime mission of our people, the continuing mercy of God, who has promised, that even in our dispersion He will not cast us off, nor break the covenant made with our fathers. We stand here as the connecting link between the past and the future. To the past we recur with feelings of pride mingled with sadness; to the future we look with never-fading hope. There was a time, when the stern realities of life assumed so depressing and crushing an aspect for the Israelite, as to leave him no other resource but his patient trust in God and the hope of brighter days. It is a remarkable fact, that our name is associated with the destinies and the history of almost every nation that ever existed, whilst our religion, taking its rise in the cradle of mankind, and sending forth its branches to the ends of the earth, may be termed the *religion of history*. May others claim the host and the power, we rest contented with the spirit. "For not by hosts, nor by power, is the salvation of mankind to be accomplished, but through my spirit, saith the Eternal." Who can deny the potent agency of Israel's religion, directly and indirectly, in the civilization, the moral and religious training of man? The sanctuary, which is this day dedicated to its holy purpose, affords a new guarantee for the perpetuity of our faith; and, in the fulness of our hearts, we may well exclaim with the psalmist, "This is the day which the Lord hath appointed, we will rejoice and be glad thereon!"

But this deep and joyous interest, which we all feel in the completion of this temple, must not grow cold or wane, but receive a new stimulus from this very hour. The *outward* structure is finished, but the *inward* structure, the edification of the soul, begins anew this day. With the act of dedication we lay the corner-stone to the spiritual fabric of holiness, which we are called upon to raise within this house, and which is to sanctify us before God. The object of this temple is, therefore, fully expressed in the words of Scripture, which shall serve as our text, אין זה כי אם בית אלהים וזה שער השמים "This is none other but a house of God and this is the gate of heaven." Gen. xxviii. 17.

Far be it from us to suppose, that we could rear a temple, and be it ever so spacious, that is to serve as a special abode for the Almighty; we have no such gross and material notions of the Deity. We pray with Solomon, "Behold the heavens, and the heavens of heavens do not contain Thee; how much less this house we have built." We exclaim with Isaiah, "Holy, holy, holy is the Lord Zebaoth, the whole earth is full of his glory!" Indeed the patriarch Jacob, who first employed the term "house of God" in our text, applied it to no structure made of human hands. In a moment of pious inspiration he designated thereby the awful spot, where God had appeared and promised to him his heavenly protection. This is precisely the case with us. We call this place a house of God, because we are here impressed with a deeper awe of God's majesty; because His divine promises here speak loudest to our hearts; because we are here more strongly reminded of His omnipotence; because here the thought of His goodness and holiness thrills most powerfully through our souls; because, in fine, as "the gate of heaven," to our imagination it appears to stand on the confines of heaven and earth, that are thus blended together in the light of eternal truth. As the house of God it shall sanctify our whole life and develop the divine attributes of our nature.

The temple is primaily a house of prayer, כי ביתי בית תפלה יקרא "For my house, says God through Isaiah, shall be called a house of prayer." Here we shall praise God in the assembly of the devout, shall pay our vows to the Most High, shall offer to Him the sacrifices of our adoration and gratitude. Here we shall celebrate the Sabbaths and festivals of the Lord and learn to distinguish between the holy and the profane. Here we shall discard from our thoughts our secular pursuits, our cares and our diversions, our hatreds and our envies, and apply ourselves to the improvement of our mind and the ennobling of our heart. Here we shall draw from the fountain of life, the word of God, those laws and precepts, those principles and maxims, which man must observe, in order to enjoy happiness here and to hope for salvation hereafter. Here, in the presence of God, we shall form resolutions of amendment, that will never be broken, and our faith in God shall increase in purity and strength from day to day.

But the prophet significantly adds, לכל העמים "to all the nations." The prayers offered, the service performed here, must not be a closed book, but intelligible to all, to the Israelite as well as to the Gentile. We have nothing to conceal. Our religious doctrines need only be known, to win the hearts of all. If Solomon at the dedication of the temple already prayed, "But also to the stranger, who is not of thy people Israel, who will come and pray in this house, mayest thou listen in heaven, and grant his petition"— how much greater is our duty, so to conduct our worship, that all who come may understand and feel, that the name of the Eternal is called upon *this* temple, and that it is a house of God!" There was a time, when our fathers had to hide from the public gaze; when the believers in the One and only God, persecuted by prejudice, fanaticism and intolerance, were not permitted openly to assemble for public worship, but were obliged to perform their divine service in sequestered localities, in fear and trembling. That time has happily passed in all civilized countries, never existed for us here, in Freedom's happy home. Everywhere throughout the length and breadth of these States magnificent temples are reared aloft, at the side of churches, in honor of the God of Israel, as enduring monuments of Equal Liberty and Freedom of Conscience. These temples, therefore, must reflect, not only in their exterior beauty, but in their inward appointments the march of enlightenment, the light of progress, the sublime spirit of religion.

If, therefore, as you have resolved, the Divine service in this temple shall not consist "in mere lip-work, the acquired precepts of men," words and ceremonies without sense and meaning, but shall engage the mind and heart, and leave a salutary impression for active life; if you here worship God in sincerity and truth; if your soul rises on the solemn tones of the organ and the sacred notes of psalmody towards heaven to draw strength and comfort for its life upon earth; if these lofty arches suggest to you the consciousness of your lofty, heaven-aspiring destiny, of your high dignity as men and moral beings, of your grateful recognition of the goodness of our Heavenly Father; if the architectural harmony displayed here impresses you with the wished-for harmony of your own life; if these finished proportions lead you, to strive for that perfection enjoined in the Divine command, תמים תהיה עם ה' אלהיך, "Thou shalt be perfect with the Lord thy God;" if, in fine, in your aggregate capacity as a congregation, you will be distinguished by works of piety, of love and humanity, even as this temple is conspicuous above other edifices—then, indeed, may you exclaim, "Let us rejoice, when they say, we will go into the house of God, for it is none other but a house of God, and this is the gate of heaven!"

And this house of God shall be called a house of prayer for all nations! Twenty-five centuries ago did the voice of inspiration proclaim this heavenly message, which has only gained strength with the change of times and the lapse of ages. Israel's religion alone is capable of furnishing the basis, upon which mankind may unite, the banner around which all the families of man may gather. It is founded upon no inexplicable mystery, embodies no doctrines that are repugnant to reason, enjoins no commands at which humanity may revolt. Its truths flow directly from the eternal fountain, and will ever remain the living springs of salvation. One God, the Father of all! One humanity, His children all!. An immortal spirit animating every human being!—Moral liberty the inalienable birth-right of every man!—Justification by our own works!—Can we conceive of a creed more sublime or more worthy of universal acceptance? And this is the creed of the Jewish religion, that is so often derided, and of the Jewish people, that have been so long, and in many bigoted and semi-civilized countries, are still sorely persecuted. This is the divine revelation kindled by the spirit of God in the spirit of man, and of which Israel has been the faithful depositary throughout the chequered phases of its existence. Silently, but effec. tually have these heavenly truths been cherished and cultivated under the weight of oppression, in the shades of compulsory seclusion—boldly, fearlessly do we proclaim them under the benign sway of liberty, and challenge the scrutiny of enlightened free-men. And although the prevailing diversities of creed preclude the prospect of an early religious fraternization, yet we undeviatingly cling to the conviction, that a day will arrive, " when the earth shall be full of knowledge of the Lord as the waters cover the sea, and the Lord will be acknowledged One and His name be One."

The "house of God," shall not only strengthen our faith in the Holy One, not only inculcate truth, but shall indelibly impress on our souls those principles of justice and love, which are ever to guide our conduct, our dealings with the world at large. The sanctification of life, which is the principal aim of our religion, can only be attained by the faithful execution of our moral duties, as taught by the word of God. Justice and love are the two adamantine pillars, upon which the welfare of society, upon which the peace of communities and of nations, is securely established. Acts of injustice, by which the eternal boundaries are removed and the rights of our neighbors infringed, are the sources of unhappiness and of the hatred, which alienates man from man, צדק תרדף ‎צדק, " Justice, only justice shalt thou pursue," is the admonition of the first and greatest prophet to his age and to all succeeding generations. Our temple emphatically teaches this lesson. Whenever we enter its hallowed precincts, we are reminded, that it is dedicated to the God of justice, and the beautiful words of the psalmist must occur to our minds, " Lord, who may sojourn in Thy tent, who may dwell upon Thy holy mountain? He who walks uprightly and who works divine justice!"— Our faith in, our reliance upon divine justice, taught and fortified in the house of God, would be empty sounds, if they did not stimulate us, to sanctify our lives by deeds of justice and righteousness.

But simple justice would be cold and dead, if it were not warmed and animated by *love*. The pious love to God and, through God, to all men will be developed and fostered in this house. It is our religious home, where we appear as children of our universal Father. Outside of this temple we meet with those diversified relations of human society, with those unavoidable distinctions of wealth, of position and of education, which are towering icebergs between man and man, and coldly separate the hearts. But here in the light of religion, before the sun of the truth, that One God has created us, that we have all *one* Father—here the icy walls melt away and the cold barriers are levelled to the ground. Here, in the house of the One and Only God, which leads to the gate of heaven, we are forced to acknowledge, that, as we shall one day be equals in the realm of eternity, so we are equals here before God, and the only distinction that is valid and true, is "the distinction between the righteous and the wicked, between him who serves God and him who serves Him not." Our very prayer can only then be of value, if the heart is free from hatred and the prayer is the expression of genuine love. The contemplation of divine love, which embraces every human being, awakens this love to God and to our fellow-man in our souL

When you, my brothers, my sisters, enjoy prosperous days, when happy events embellish your lot, and you enter the house of God, to thank him for his benefits—is it not upon the altar of divine love, that you pour out the libation of your gratitude? And when your horizon should be darkened, when dangers are impending, when affliction shrouds your soul in mourning and gloom, and you hasten to the house of God, to supplicate his help and comfort—is it not the divine love, upon which you count for aid and deliverance in the hour of trial and distress? And when remorse for an evil deed gnaws at your heart, and you humbly petition for pardon, is it not the love and mercy of God, on which you base your hope for forgiveness? Prayer then is the mediator, the electric current, between the love of man and the love of God. And this love shall be the abiding sentiment of our life. Hence it is, that an ancient teacher declares ואהבת לרעך כמוך זה כלל גדול בתורה, "Thou shalt love thy neighbor as thyself, is the highest principle of the law." But not only our religion, but every creed which claims to be divine, adapted to the wants of man and founded upon a rational basis, must place this law at the very head of its duties; and every house of God, which shall be recognized as a truly religious institution, must foster and cultivate in its prayers and teachings and in all its exercises of worship, sentiments and feelings of love.

No graver error can be perpetrated by men, farther they can not stray from the right path, a more grievous sin they can not commit than perverting the Word, which God has sent into the world for the promotion of love and peace, into the means of hatred and hostility, of oppression and persecution, by teaching and preaching in the consecrated places, where love and peace should be cherished and fostered, hatred and persecution against those, who hold different religious convictions. This temple will not be thus perverted. The prayers and hymns which will here be offered, are invocations to our heavenly Father to grant his blessings not only to us, but to all his children; the symbols and ceremonies exhibited here are designed to remind us, that God has destined all the inhabitants of the earth to holiness and salvation; and the word of God, which will be read from this desk and interpreted from this pulpit, will ever breathe the spirit of peace and good-will to all the children of man.

Truly then may we apply the words of our text to this temple, "This is none other but a house of God, and this is the gate of heaven!"

V.

ADDRESS

Delivered at the Laying of the Corner-Stone

OF

TEMPLE SINAI,

OF NEW ORLEANS,

Sunday, Nov. 19th, 1871.

WE are engaged in a holy work. The corner-stone of a new Jewish house of worship is about to be laid, and we have assembled to witness this symbolical, time-honored ceremony and to testify by our presence the deep interest we feel in the erection of this edifice. Upon this foundation, it has been resolved, to rear a house devoted to the worship of the Most High, the Creator and Governor of the universe, the Father of all mankind, the Guardian of Israel—a temple worthy of the name we bear, and the religion we profess. With the completion of this edifice, the recently organized congregation, " Temple Sinai,", will possess a religious home, wherein to assemble from "new moon to new moon, and from Sabbath to Sabbath," in order to foster the eternal truths of Judaism, pure and undefiled in spirit and in form, and to pour out the inmost feelings of their hearts in praise, in thanks, and in supplication before the eternal, omnipotent. and all-merciful Ruler of the universe, who has guarded and directed the destinies of Israel from Sinai's world-redeeming revelation to the present day, and whose promised divine guardianship will endure to all eternity.

The occasion forcibly calls to mind the prophetic words of Isaiah (XVIII. 16): "*Therefore, thus saith the Lord Eternal, behold, I have laid in Zion as a foundation a stone, a tried stone, a precious corner-stone, well founded: the faithful will not hastily waver.*"

Sinai and Zion! Two names of the most thrilling interest, of the deepest importance, of the most salutary influence to Israel and to mankind. They are the mountains of the Lord, from which heavenly truth gushed forth and spread in ever-widening circles. They are the fountain-heads of the religious and moral culture of the human race, the elevated points, where heaven and earth are happily blended, the divine and human harmoniously united. Sinai and Zion are household-words, wherever God is worshipped in spirit and in truth, for " from Sinai the Lord shone forth, at his right hand a fiery law"—"and from Zion comes forth the law and the word of God from Jerusalem."

Sinai and Zion! What hallowed associations cluster around these two names, whose pristine brightness has remained undimmed in the march of many centuries and the wide area of the earth's surface. They are forever synonyms of light and truth. Even from this distant spot in the New World we cannot help contemplating them with a solemn veneration and sacred delight, as their outlines and their historical importance rise before our mental vision. The stone, laid as a foundation in Zion, was the imperishable block, hewn from Sinai's adamantine quarry. However fierce the storm of human passions, however violent the onslaught of the misconceived zeal, engendered by blind fanaticism, it was too firmly imbedded, ever to be dislodged. It was "a tried stone," designed and fashioned by the hand of Omnipotence, and upon its foundation the temple of truth and of love, the temple of knowledge of the One and only God, the Father of all—and of the fraternal bonds that should unite all his children, was to be reared in all its holiness and glory for the happiness of man. It was "a precious corner-stone," exceeding all worldly grandeur and material wealth, as it constitutes the immovable basis of moral purity and greatness of soul. Whoever built upon this stone—his structure was well founded; whoever stood "firm and faithful, did not hastily waver," but from the midst of temporary gloom and harrassing trials he looked forward, with the eye of hope, to a bright and peaceful future.

"The tried stone, the precious corner-stone, laid as a sure foundation in Zion," is identical with the corner-stone of Judaism. To speak without metaphor, Judaism is founded upon the belief in the absolute unity of God, in the recognition and worship of the One spiritual, all-wise, all-merciful and omnipotent Creator and Ruler of the universe, who has created man in His own image by endowing him with a soul, capable of comprehending this truth, of unfolding its inherent intellectual and moral powers, and destined for immortality. This truth, proclaimed from Sinai and ratified at Zion for the benefit of all mankind, "in order, as Solomon prays, that all the people of the earth may know, that the Lord is God and there is none else"—is neither enveloped in mysteries, nor disfigured by types. It is in beautiful harmony with human reason and directly appeals, in tender and soothing accents, to the human heart. It is the perpetual revelation of the eternal, immutable, ever-living God to the spirit of man in every age. Before the heavenly light of this truth, the lurid flames of idolatry and superstition, and the meteoric flashes of atheism must pale their ineffectual fires. The standard of religious truth, thus unfurled by Israel, will be held aloft, until all the families of the earth will flock around it for their blessing.

The belief in the One eternal God and Father, as taught by Judaism, has proved, directly and indirectly, the most potent factor in the advancement of true civilization. It has steadily promoted the moral progress, elevated the mind and refined the heart of man. It has shed its heavenly light on, and clearly defined the eternal principles of justice, of liberty, of brotherly love. At a time, when darkness covered the nations, when heathenism with its flagrant vices and gross aberrations brutalized mankind, the law of Sinai inculcated as practical rules for government and for life, " you shall have but one law and one judgment for the native and for the stranger," *i. e.* you shall mete out equal justice to all ; " you shall neither vex nor oppress the stranger," but accord him the full measure of liberty which you enjoy; "thou shalt love the stranger as thyself"—a command which appears as a complementary enforcement of the comprehensive moral precept, " Thou shalt love thy neighbor as thyself."

And these principles were compressed into one beautiful sentence, by the last of Zion's prophets, "Have we not all One Father ? hath not *one* God created us ? Why then should we act treacherously one against the other ?" Yes, the belief in one God, who embraces all mankind in His paternal love and wise providence, must strengthen the sentiment in the human heart, to regard and treat every human being as the child of God, as a brother. Upon this belief, therefore, "as the tried and precious cornerstone," the world-wide temple of humanity is destined to rise, slowly but surely, in its grand and lofty proportions.

The memories and associations clustering around

Sinai and Zion were never dissevered from Israel's history; they are not simply the dead-letter record of the past, but are enshrined as imperishable legacies in the hearts of the people selected by God as the missionaries of divine truth; they come to us to-day, enforced not only by the faith and constancy, the virtues and sacrifices and sufferings of a long line of ancestry, but by the lessons and experiences of the times in which we live; and we are resolved, not with any feeble expectation or faltering hope only, but with a firm persuasion and assured trust and faith, to send them down all sparkling and blazing to the remotest posterity. In the spiritual empire of religious truth "the sceptre has not departed from Judah." The two great religious systems, which ostensibly govern the civilized world, Christianity and Mohamedanism, have sprung from Judaism; whatever is sound and vigorous and fruitful in their constitutions has been drawn from, and is quickened by her life-sustaining maternal bosom. Judaism, like the sun, is resplendent in its own light, while its planetary orbs shine in a borrowed effulgence drawn from its primitive fountain.

Truth remains unalterably the same. It is the signet of God, stamped upon nature and history, upon matter and spirit, eternal and immutable like God himself. The principles and doctrines of Judaism, therefore, with their divine charter of Sinai and their tried corner-stone of Zion, must be true to all eternity. No expediency, no compromise, no sophistry can shake their permanent validity. If the recognition and worship of the Holy One was ever true (and this fact must be universally conceded), if at any time it was the precious corner-stone of genuine faith and morality, then the doctrine of One God, who exists peerless and alone in His divine majesty, must remain true, as long as the mind of man is capable of reasoning and the heart of man susceptible of truth.

It was the peculiar, heaven-ordained mission of Israel, to be the custodian, the propagator, the ever-existing witness of this truth, the Messiah of nations, the light of the gentiles. To this end it was appointed, by divine mandate, "as a Kingdom of priests and a holy nation;" to this end it has been preserved throughout the checquered events of history, amidst the crumbling of thrones and the crash of empires, bravely sustaining the fierce and prolonged storms of intolerance, of fanaticism and persecution that raged around its devoted head. Beyond the cloudy horizon of the gloomy present, it ever discerned the bright dawn of a serene future, "when the knowledge of God will cover the earth, as the waters cover the sea." For although religious truth has advanced by slow and measured stages, yet its dominion has visibly expanded, and its future realization, though remote, is sure and certain. In the words of the prophets Isaiah and Micah, "And it shall come to pass in the last days, that the mountain of the Lord's house shall be firmly established on the top of the mountains, and shall be exalted above the hills; and unto it shall flow all the nations. And many people shall go and say, Come ye, let us go up to the mountain of the Lord, to the house of the God of Jacob; that he may teach us of his ways, and we may walk in his paths." Until that time, when all mankind will know and worship the One and only God, Judaism, the venerable and faithful mother, is willing and anxious to live in amity, in brotherhood, and in peace with her numerous offspring of variously apparelled daughters. Synagogue and Church, though differing in matters of faith, are yet in perfect agreement on the moral law of the Bible. Upon this broad platform we stand as a united band of brothers, inspired by a common duty, to work for the improvement and happiness of our common race.

There is nothing more wonderful in the history of the human race than the way, in which the religious and moral ideal of Sinai has traversed the lapse of ages, acquiring a new strength and beauty with each advance of civilization, and infusing its beneficent influence into every sphere of thought and action. The moral development of mankind is sure to progress to its destined goal by the assimilating and attractive influence of this grand ideal.

In the present aspect of the world it devolves upon Judaism, to present the standard of this ideal to the public eye, in all its attractiveness and perfection, stripped of mere speculative doctrines and ritualistic observances, which in former periods of history were deemed necessary for its preservation. True religion sanctions no doctrine which collides with our reason or our moral sense, no speculative theories or ceremonies, which, without being opposed to conscience, are at least wholly beyond its sphere.

Guided by these principles and considerations the movement of modern reform in Judaism was inaugurated, and has steadily gained the fervent sympathy and support of numerous faithful adherents. It is a plant of spontaneous growth, emanating from within and not from without, and hence must thrive and prosper. Reform means rational progress; reform means life; reform means enlightened conviction; reform means sublime devotion to the holiest interests and to the grand ideal ever cherished by Judaism. Under the banner of reform Judaism has revived from its lethargy, has put forth its native energy and vigor, and bids fair to realize its glorious future. Directed at first to the abatement of crying abuses in the synagogue it has steadily extended its sphere and its regenerating influence is now felt in every department of Jewish life.

It has breathed order into chaos, chased away the dense clouds of superstition that darkened the religious horizon, and purified the spiritual atmosphere of Israel. And these grand results have been achieved, "not by force, not by violence, but by the power of truth."

Members of "Temple Sinai!" Words are inadequate to convey to you my emotions of deep-felt gratitude for having called me from the distant North, to express the ideas and sentiments, which the act, in which we are engaged, naturally inspires. It affords me a holy satisfaction, to witness the substantial evidences on your part, that the seeds, which your former teacher and guide has sown in singleness of purpose and purity of motive, have not fallen on barren soil. You have undertaken a holy and glorious work. The corner-stone is about to be laid to-day—the temple will soon be erected and afford, under divine providence, a lasting monument to your noble efforts. Great, no doubt, were the exertions, great the sacrifices, which it has hitherto cost you; and still the work is yet in its inception, and great, no doubt, will yet be the sacrifices for its completion.

"Be strong, therefore, and of good courage, fear not, nor be ye afraid." Persevere in your holy zeal. "Remain steadfast and faithful, do not hastily waver." Continue to act, as you have hitherto done, in union and harmony, with courage and perseverance, and all difficulties will be easily surmounted, a triumphant success will crown your efforts.

As your fathers, the whole people of Israel, were assembled in the days of yore at the base of Mount Sinai and listened to the words of revelation, which since then constitute the corner-stone of the temple of humanity, so are you assembled this day around the corner-stone of "Temple Sinai," renewing your allegiance to God, determined to remain faithful to the spirit of his holy law. But unlike your fathers, you are not encamped in a bleak, inhospitable desert, nor surrounded by hostile, barbarian tribes, but are free citizens of a great and glorious Republic, settlers of a thriving and noble State, residents of a fair city, whose changing fortunes could not affect the high-minded impulses, the liberal and generous spirit, by which its inhabitants were ever distinguished. Indeed, the numerous attendance of our fellow-citizens of other creeds, some to testify their interest and sympathy as spectators, others by active participation in the exercises of the hour, practically illustrates the beautiful line of the sacred bard, "Behold how good, and how pleasant it is, for brethren to dwell together in unity!"

Let the corner-stone, therefore, be laid with the accustomed rites by the worthy brotherhood, whose motto is *Light, Truth* and *Charity;* whose principles and practice are in full harmony with the principles and practice of Judaism.

In the name of God, we solemnly dedicate this cornerstone, upon which the sacred edifice is to rest. May the "Temple Sinai" realize the fervent anticipations of its founders, become a fountain of holy and blessed influence, a visible embodiment and messianic teacher of the two cardinal principles of true religion. "*Allegiance to God-Good will to man!*"

VI.

SERMON

Delivered at the Dedication of the

TEMPLE AHAWATH CHESED,

OF NEW YORK,

Friday, April 19th, 1872.

" In order that all the nations of the earth may know that the Lord is the true God, none else." (*I. K.* VIII, 60.)

WITH these words King Solomon concluded his addresses and his prayers at the dedication of the Temple, which marked an era in Israel's history. These words have an infinitely wider application than the place and the occasion on which they were uttered. They not only designate the object of every Jewish house of worship, but most emphatically express the end and object of the Jewish religion itself. Ever since the divine promise was made to Abraham, " In thee and in thy seed all the families of the earth shall be blessed!" ever since Israel received the glorious appointment, " You shall be unto me a kingdom of priests and a holy nation;" Judaism has strenuously labored, in the various phases of its checkered history, to realise this promise, to act in the spirit of this appointment, to the end, " that all the nations of the earth may know that the Lord is the true God, none else."

In dedicating, therefore, this magnificent temple to the worship of the Most High, the Creator of the universe, the Father of all mankind, under conditions and surroundings so different from those which existed at the time of Solomon, we are forcibly reminded of the eternal, indefeasible validity of Israel's mission, "to be a covenant of the people, a light of the nations," לברית עם לאור גוים (Isa. 42, 6). However great the change which our position to the outer world has undergone in the course of centuries, our peculiar relation to God, as the lineal descendants and heirs of those, who were divinely commissioned as the depositaries of the eternal religious truth, as the custodians of pure morality, is as patent this day as at any previous period of our history to every impartial, unprejudiced mind. The cardinal doctrine of our faith and of true religion in general, "Hear, O Israel, the Lord our God is One!" is still repeated in our houses of worship with undiminished fervor, and the decalogue still regarded and revered as the corner-stone of morality and social well-being. And, however much of the promised divine blessing may already have been imparted to the families of man through our agency, still our task is not finished, our mission not accomplished untill "the whole earth is full of the knowledge of God, as the waters cover the sea"—until the spirit of God, the spirit of wisdom and knowledge, the spirit of justice and benevolence, the spirit of counsel and of genuine fear of God will animate the whole human race, and harmony, peace and love will unite all mankind into one sacred bond of brotherhood. Notwithstanding, therefore, all the political, social, material, and intellectual changes, which have taken place, and which have transformed the aspect of the world, our present relation to God is the same as in the days of Abraham, of Moses and of Solomon. In this respect the words of the prophet are literally verified:

I, the Lord, do not change, and ye, sons of Jacob, shall never cease. (Mal. 3, 6.)

Now the question arises, what are the consequences of our changed outward relations to the world, and our unchanged, spiritual relation to God? In other words, how can the duties attached to either be made to harmonize?

The proper illustration of this subject is, in my opinion, alike interesting to Israelites and non-Israelites, and is eminently suited to the truth-inspiring act, in which we are engaged.

The twenty-first verse of the fifty-ninth chapter of Isaiah shall serve our text:

"And as for me, this is my covenant with them, saith the Lord, my spirit that is upon thee, and my words, which I have put in thy mouth, shall not depart out of thy mouth, nor out of the mouth of thy children, nor out of the mouth of thy children's children, saith the Lord, from henceforth and to all eternity."

The history of Israel is characterized by three distinct periods: that of the patriarchs, of the political independence as a nation, and of the dispersion.

In "looking to the rock from whence we were hewn," we find that Abraham had a pure conception of God and His all-wise providence; that he fostered a rational faith in God; that he practised sublime virtue and piety, by which alone the temporal and eternal happiness of the individual and of the race can be secured. The source of blessing thus welling in Abraham, should not be suffered to dry up, but was destined to become through him and his posterity the ultimate property of all mankind. Hence it followed, as a necessary consequence, that his descendants should cultivate and preserve this blessing, or this faith, in its purity, that through them, it might be communicated to the families of the earth.

The patriarchs, in their simple patriarchal family-life, were able to foster this faith, without requiring a distinct, exclusive relation to the outward world. They could enjoy and cultivate this blessing in any country, in any relation of life, under various political and social conditions, and by their simple but sublime faith, by their simple but heart-felt worship, by their pious walk before God, be paragons of holiness and shining models to their contemporaries. In this period, therefore, with one single exception, we meet with no revelation of specific laws, with no institution of distinct ceremonies and symbols. It was enough for the patriarchs to exhibit a life distinguished by a pure, firm faith in the One and only God, and by the brightest virtues of humanity.

But when the descendants of Abraham had increased to a numerous people, other methods were required to preserve the divine blessing inherited from the patriarchs for the benefit of the human race. "Delivered from the iron furnace of Egypt," they had outgrown the simple family relation, without yet possessing the prerequisites for national independence. In order to accomplish their inherited mission as custodians and propagators of religious truth, Divine Wisdom put them in possession of the promised land; enacted laws and statutes, civil and political, adapted for the exigencies of their independent national existence; established a mode of public worship, symbols and ceremonies in keeping with the spirit of the age—but all this with the specific object of creating a national unity, of blending and amalgamating the pure faith in God, the pure religous idea, with the very life-blood of the people.

But who does not perceive that all these acquisitions and developments—the possession of a country, the political, agragrian, civil and ecclesiastical institutions, the sacrifices and levitical orders—were but radiations of the grand central focus, whose light was increased by their reflecting beams. Who does not perceive that all these institutions and laws, which fill the best part of the Pentateuch and have mostly become inoperative, were established by Divine Wisdom, to realize Israel's grand mission as the depositaries and channel of the divine blessing.

Looking through the vista of thousands of years, the ancient commonwealth of Israel apears to us as a sunny, fruitful oasis in the midst of the benighted, sterile desert of paganism.

We have arrived at the third period. When eighteen hundred years ago, under the providence of God, all these institutions were subverted; when the Jewish State was dissolved, the political organization, the civil and ecclesiastical constitution, the sacerdotal and levitical orders, and the sacrificial worship, were overwhelmed by the ruins of the Temple, Israel ceased to be a body politie and returned to its primitive family relation. The remaining fragments of the people were scattered to all parts of the globe. and the single families united in more or less numerous religious communities or congregations, held together by the bond of their common inherited faith.

What has been, and what is now, our relation to God under this changed state of things?

We occupy the same relation to our Heavenly Father, which we erst sustained, before it pleased God to create our nationality, to lead us into the promised land, to form us into a body politic, with distinct civil, political and ecclesiastical institutions, in a word, before he invested us with that peculiar, exclusive character which, for the time of its continuance, was deemed the most efficient means of realizing our mission: *to preserve intact the world-redeeming religious truth.* We have returned to the same relation to God, which the patriarchs occupied in the days of old. The covenant of God with Abraham, renewed and amplified on Sinai with the whole house of Israel, has never been abrogated or superseded, but applies to us in its original force and significance. As the seed and heirs of the great Patriarch it is still our duty, not to suffer the source of the divine blessing to become extinct or adulterated within us, but to be up and doing, in order that the salutary rays of the true knowledge and worship of God pour their saving light on all the families of the earth. All the outward conditions and insignia of our political and national existence were no integral parts of the divine covenant, but simply constituted the means of its preservation during a long series of centuries. The covenant itself is still unchangeably the same: That through Abraham and his seed all the families of the earth shall be blessed. And this is precisely the idea expressed in our text, "And as for me, this is my covenant with them, saith the Lord, my spirit that is upon thee, and my words, which I have put in thy mouth, shall not depart out of thy mouth, nor out of the mouth of thy children, nor out of the mouth of thy children's children, saith the Lord, from henceforth and unto all eternity."

From what has been advanced it will thus appear, that in our present condition our relation to God is no longer that of a peculiar people or nation, in a political sense of these terms. We occupy the same ground which the patriarchs occupied: we are distinguished as *Jewish families*. Our peculiar relation to God only consists in our peculiar mission: To foster the pure faith in the Holy One by the worship of His Holy Name, in spirit and in truth, and by a virtuos and moral conduct. And this our peculiar mission is not to be regarded as involving sacred obligations generally incumbent upon man, but as the special appointment by God of ourselves and our children, to preserve the spiritual treasures confided to Israel in all their purity, that they may become the perennial source of inexhaustible blessings to all the children of man. We can not renounce this peculiar relation to God without annihilating our identity, without ceasing to be Israelites, without severing ourselves from a long line of ancestry, creating a gap which can never be closed, and bidding adieu for ever to our parental home. We can not renounce this peculiar relation to God, until the hope, which springs from its stem like an ever-blooming branch, until the hope, which, like a radiant star, shines through the gloomy night of our history, shall be realized: the hope, that pure faith in God, genuine piety, virtue and brotherly love will one day become the heritage of all mankind.

But our peculiar relation to God by no means implies a peculiar relation to our fellow-men. Divested of all specifically political and national characteristics, our families constituting integral portions of the people of the various countries of our birth or adoption, we cordially mingle and earnestly desire to cultivate a friendly intercourse with our fellow-citizens of other creeds, in all secular and human relations; and this was precisely the condition of the patriarchs. In all human and worldly affairs they worked hand in hand with their contemporaries; they only differed in their faith, in their knowledge and worship of God, in their uncompromising virtue. In this respect they were far in advance of their age. In the patriarchal times, religion was not yet united with the State—with us Israelites religion has been totally severed from the State for the last eighteen hundred years.

But it may be objected that this view of our present position and duties was opposed to the principle of progress which we cherish, and of which this temple shall afford renewed testimony and a glorious monument. It may be asked, can it be possible, that for you alone Moses should have lived and taught in vain—that his laws, his statutes and his ordinances should have been ephemeral institutions—that the prophets and God-inspired men, whom Israel has produced, should have left no impress of their teachings—that all the trials, the experiences and the developments of history should only serve to place you on the same ground which your fathers occupied many hundred years before Israel was created a nation? Is not this retrogression rather than progress?

These objections, however plausible they seem, can readily be answered. True it is, we firmly and unreservedly adhere to the religion taught by Moses, and fervently declare: תורה צוה לנו משה מורשה קהלת יעקב, "The law which Moses commanded us is the inheritance of the congregation of Jacob." The great prophet has not lived in vain for us, and the lessons and influence of the God-inspired men, who taught in his spirit, are not lost on our minds and hearts, although we are no longer the sole possessors of their doctrines, their ideas and their teachings. The powerful stream of religious truth, taking its rise with Abraham, and increasing in volume and purity under Moses and the prophets, has sent forth two great and mighty branches, which have in part diffused the divine blessing in many directions. But in order to properly appreciate our present relation, it is necessary to distinguish between the *Mosaic Polity*, that is, the civil constitution of the people of Israel in the shape of a theocracy, and the *Mosaic Religion*, that is, the revelation of the Divine Providence and government of the universe. The first, with all its laws, statutes and ordinances, has lost its practical value; the latter constitutes the unchangeable, imperishable scope of Israel's existence. The peculiar polity was necessitated by the conditions of the age, to secure the perpetuity of religious truth. It was the means, and not the end. Hence the Jewish religion survived the Jewish State. The political institutions, the civil and ceremonial enactments contained in the Pentateuch, had a temporary and local value, and could never be designed to stand forever; but the *Religion*, for the preservation of which they were instituted, should, through Israel, become the law of the world.

And for this higher destiny the law of Moses made ample provision. It not only enjoined on the people obedience to God as the national Ruler, but also pure, self-sacrificing love—with all the heart, all the soul, and all the might—towards God as the Father; not only the observance of the civil and ceremonial laws, but also of the moral precepts of virtue and holiness; not only respect for the person and property of the neighbor, but also disinterested love for the native and stranger. The civil and ecclesiastical laws were but ancillary to the establishment of *religious truth*—i. e., the purest conception of God and his holy will; the sanctification of man by holy sentiments and virtuous deeds; the diffusion of justice in its highest sense, and love in its sublimest scope. While, therefore, the laws in their outward form were dependent upon existing conditions, and had to stand or fall with these ever-changing conditions, the *spirit*, which called them into being, is unchangeable and imperishable, because it is the spirit of religion, the spirit of God, which is immutable, which retains its eternal creative vigor and freshness amidst all the changes of the outward relations of life.

And it is this spirit, and not the letter, which we cherish and revere. Not in their concrete outward form, but in their spirit, are the institutions of Moses and the revelations of the prophets, our eternal, inexhaustible sources of instruction and never failing guides. But it would be an error to assume, that with the destruction of its political nationality Israel had forfeited Divine grace, had fallen from its high estate of being the divinely-appointed teacher of genuine religious truths for all mankind. Our status during the dispersion, similar to that occupied by the patriarchs, is therefore no retrogression, but actual progress. Our relation to God is unchanged. The realization of our mission is facilitated by the law of Moses and the teachings of the prophets, which, in their spirit, constitute the inalienable inheritance of the congregation of Jacob.

This conclusion is not the result of a speculative theory, but is borne out by our long eventful history, in which God has ever revealed himself to us, which has planted the faith in the benign providence of God still more deeply into our hearts, and enabled us, more fully to comprehend our relation to God, our peculiar mission and our general duties to man. There is no people on earth that can better learn its destiny and its powers from its history than Israel can learn from its own; and in order to realize our present position, it is necessary to comprehend the revelation of God in our history. Through its mouth God speaks to us as solemnly as he once did through the mouth of Moses. With the annihilation of our political independence God himself has reduced us to our present stage, to faithfully execute the sacred commission which he entrusted to our hands, and to guard the precious treasure of religious truth, not as a nation among the nations, but as families among the families of the earth. History teaches us, that our status as Israelites is a far higher one than it was at any previous period, because it bears a purely religious character, and is separated from all political aspirations and worldly grandeur. We stand nearer to God than at any previous period, because our experiences in history have fitted us to understand, more clearly than we have ever done heretofore, the object of our mission. Our history served us as a special school, to be educated for our calling. The end of our mission is but partially gained; for as yet only a portion of mankind enjoys the promised blessing through Israel's instrumentality. Its full measure shall be realized not by worldly power and political ascendancy, but by purely spiritual means and moral agencies.

Ever since our dispersion Judaism has been completely separated from the State, has assumed its pristine purity as a religion of the mind and heart, of conviction and of feeling. We know, better than ever before, that as Israelites it is our duty to worship the One and only God, and to love Him with all our heart, with all our soul, and with all our might. We know, that as men we are sincerely devoted, in common with our fellow-citizens of other creeds, to the country which we claim as our own; that it is our sacred obligation, faithfully and cheerfully to perform all the duties of citizenship and of humanity, to love every man as our neighbor, as our brother, as ourselves.

It is well to define thus publicly and solemnly our relation to the outward world, in the light in which it is viewed by ourselves, since it frequently happens, that, when Jews and Judaism are touched upon in the pulpit or the press, intelligent divines and enlightened writers speak of the present generations of Israel as belonging to the past, as constituting a peculiar people with peculiar political aspirations. It is well to show, that our religion simply defines our relation to God; that in our character as men, as citizens, we have no separate objects, no exclusive ends to pursue. Our religion only so far regulates our intercourse with the world, as it insists upon a moral and virtuous conduct, upon the practice of incorruptible honesty and justice, of diffusive benevolence, as the only means of securing our eternal salvation. In every other respect, our interests are identical with the interests of the country whose children we are, and for whose welfare and prosperity it is our duty to pray and to devote our best energies.

It will thus be perceived that our covenant with God is a spiritual compact, which renders it imperative upon us to see, that the spirit of God which rests upon us, which has descended upon us from the patriarchs in unbroken continuity, shall not depart from us and from our children to all eternity; that we are resolved to remain the trustees of the divine blessing, the depositaries of pure religious truth, until all divergent creeds shall have disappeared; until all the nations and all the families of the earth will know and worship the One and only God; until, throughout the earth, God will be acknowledged One and His Name One; "until all the nations of the earth will know, that the Lord is God, there is none else."

VII.

"THE SPIRIT OF GOD IN MAN,"

A SERIES OF FOUR SERMONS,

DELIVERED AT

TEMPLE EMANU-EL.

1.
Sabbath, March 2d, 1872.

"*And the Lord said unto Moses : ' Go thou up unto this mount of Abarim and see the land which I have given unto the children of Israel. And when thou hast seen it, then shalt thou also be gathered unto thy people, as Aaron thy brother hath been gathered. Because you rebelled against my order in the desert of Zin, at the quarrelling of the congregation, to sanctify me through the waters before their eyes: these are the waters of Meribah in Kadesh, in the wilderness of Zin.----And Moses spoke unto the Lord, saying, Let the Lord, the God of the spirits of all flesh, appoint a man over the congregation, who may go out before them and who may bring them in; that the Congregation of the Lord be not as a flock which have no shepherd. And the Lord said unto Moses, Take to thyself Joshua, the son of Nun, a man in whom there is spirit, and thou shalt lay they hand upon him. And thou shalt cause him to stand before Elazar the priest, and befo e all the congregation; and thou shalt give him a charge before their eyes. And thou shalt put some of thy greatness upon him; in order that all the congregation of the children of Israel may be obedient.*" Numbers XXVII, 12---20.

THE opinion has long ago been expressed, אין מוקדם ומאוחר בתורה "that the Pentateuch is not chronologically arranged." Some of its historical incidents and episodes stand in no connection with the passage immediately preceding and following, and the date of their occurence can only be ascertained by a careful examination of the Mosaic record. This absence of historical conciseness, moreover, evidently favors the conclusion, that each of the Five Books is the separate work of an independent compiler. The passage quoted as our text obviously belongs to the close of the Pentateuch.

The day approached, when Moses must die. The people, for whom he had so long cared, and whom he had so anxiously led, were now ready to enter the promised land; but he was forbidden to go in with them. His work was done; his great task was accomplished; and it only remained for him to render up his life.

Yet it was fit, that before this venerable servant of God laid down his charge, he should see *that* part of it which could be transmitted, deposited in proper hands, that he might die in the comfortable assurance, that the great work he had undertaken might be vigorously prosecuted after his death. Ever since the fatal day of Meribah, the prophet knew, that he was doomed to die, without setting the sole of his foot upon the land, which was to form the heritage of his people. But now he receives a distinct intimation, as his brother had before, that the appointed time was come and, like him, he is directed to ascend the neighboring mountain, there to render up his life. Observe well how he receives this intimation. What is the foremost thought in his mind? Nothing that concerns himself—no regret of his own; all his thought is for the welfare of the people: "Let the Eternal, the God of the spirits of all flesh, set a man over the congregation, who may go out before them, and who may go in before them, and who may lead them out, and who may bring them in; that the congregation of the Lord be not as sheep which have no no shepherd." Here is the same loftiness of spirit, rising above every thought of self—the same zeal for the honor of God,—the same devoted solicitude for the welfare of the people, which had hitherto marked his whole career. We may wade through folios of history and biography narrating the mighty deeds of warriors, statesmen and professed patriots, before we find another case equal to it in interest.

The suit of Moses was heard, and Joshua, who had already had opportunities of distinguishing himself by his faithfulness and by his courage, was directed to be solemnly inaugurated at the tabernacle as the future leader of the Hebrew host. Nothing then remained for Moses to do, but to pour out his heart before the people in lofty odes and eloquent blessings. Then he retired to the appointed mountain, that he might, before his death, survey the goodly land, in which the people were to establish that noble commonwealth, which he had so laboriously organized.

Joshua was thus solemnly appointed as his successor, and his fitness for the high and difficult office was characterized by a single word, which I propose to take as the subject of my discourse for this and the next occasion. " God said to Moses, Take Joshua, the son of Nun, a man in whom there is *spirit*." The Hebrew " רוח " and its equivalent " *spirit* " are identical both in their primary and abstract sense. רוח and spirit, in their primary sense denote " breath,, " and this being the vital function of the animal organism, רוח and spirit are employed to designate the soul of man; the intelligent, immaterial and immortal part of human beings. And thus, in its abstract sense, the term is applied in both languages to express life, ardor, fire, elevation or vehemence of mind; the essential qualities of any faculty, affection, sentiment and disposition, of virtue and vice, of good and evil. Hence the terms : spirit of truth and spirit of falsehood—spirit of love and spirit of selfishness—spirit of justice and spirit of oppression—spirit of meeknsss and spirit of pride—spirit of wisdom and spirit of folly—spirit of liberality and spirit of avarice—spirit of piety and spirit of worldliness: are current in both languages and are familiar to our ears. In order, therefore, to correctly understand the quality of the spirit by which Joshua is represented in our text as being animated, we must refer to other portions of Scripture, in order to appreciate it correctly. In the last chapter of the Pentateuch, where the circumstance is alluded to, it is said of Joshua מלא רוח חכמה that he was full of the spirit of wisdom. Joseph is praised as a man, אשר רוח אלהים בו in whom there is the spirit of God. Of Bezalel we read that God, had filled him with the spirit of God. The question, therefore, what is the spirit of God in man, which shall become the standard of our thoughts, words and actions, which shall overrule the human spirit—is naturally suggested. Let us explain by an illustration.

Standing on the crest of a mountain or in a large plain, where our eye, as far it reaches, may enjoy an unobtructed view, it invariably appears to us, as if we were standing in the centre of an immense circle at our base, and under the very central point of the hemisphere of the visible heavens, that seems to rest on the distant edges of the horizon all around us; and though we may change our position ever so often, every new standpoint we may chose will still appear to us as the center of the vast earthly circle, and the highest point of the celestial vault will seem to be directly above our head. Whatever point we may chose will seem to us the central point of the horizon. This physical phenomenon, no doubt familiar to you all, finds its analogy in the spiritual horizon of man.

Every man is naturally fond to regard himself as the

central point, around which the whole world is moving. He refers everything to *himself*, and his judgment is regulated according to the interests he individually has in any relation, circumstance or occurrence—pronouncing good what is useful, and bad what is injurious to himself. " Dear self " is his ideal ; it is, as it were, the text-book from which he draws the rules, that sway his judgment of allthings in heaven and earth.

Of course you will rarely find a person, that will confess as much. But we do not now inquire, what man is according to his own confession, but what he is, when stripped of all the guises which hypocrisy and self deception have drawn around him.

I will readily admit, that, if we were capable of beholding the soul of man in its real state, divested of all artificial guises, we would even then rarely discover selfishness, so absolute and unqualified, as to be relieved by no redeeming trait. Still this does not contradict the position assumed, but only proves that there is seldom a man to be found, who had not within him something of the spirit of God, tending to mitigate his asperities and to soften his harshness; but it is necessary to glance at the godless spirit in man, in all its unvarnished hideousness, in order to recognize, what is the true spirit of God.

Absolute, unqualified selfishness, in its full force, will in but few men continue beyond earliest childhood. It has been justly remarked that the child is the greatest egotist. It appropriates every thing to itself, has no conception of mine and thine, of duty, moral obligation and responsibility; its world is bounded by the walls of the nursery, and here it is met by persons, who only give and bestow, witont demanding a return; but as our horizon expands, and the world increases in extent to our view, in the same proportion do we learn and feel that we are by no means the centre of the universe, but only a link in the infinite chain of all created beings, and that all things are not intended for our special individual benefit, but also for the benefit of others. Yes, in the soul of the wise, the impression gains ground, that we are designed for the benefit of others and to promote the beneficent ends of Providence, which we are unable to fully comprehend. It is only when man is duly impressed with this thought, that he ceases to be בן אדם, a son of man, and becomes בן אלהים, a son of God, inasmuch as he recognizes God as the Father of all mankind; and having gained this conviction, he must recognize in every human being the child of God, equally favored, equally beloved, and equally protected by our heavenly Father. It thus appears, that only he, who holds his self-love under proper control, can worship God, in spirit and in truth, as the God of the universe; while the slave of selfishness, who lives in the contracted sphere of his own individuality, constitutes, as far as in him lies, "a state within the state of God," and will sooner or later rebel against divine government and Providence.

There have been philosophers, who have tried to reduce the whole range of human duties to a single comprehensive proposition. One said, that the cardinal duty from which all other duties flow, was the strict adherence to truth. This proposition is by no means incorrect, as there is scarcely a sin which is not, directly or indirectly, based upon a lie. Others maintained, that the cardinal, all-comprehensive duty was to take God as the model of our life and action. Who will deny, that this proposition, too, contains a truth, as soon as we have ascertained, which attributes of God we shall imitate; otherwise there would be people, who would choose to imitate God's uncompromising justice and absolute power rather than his infinite love and mercy. Others have advanced still other theories upon this subject.

But we Israelites have no need of these philosophical niceties and distinctions. We acknowledge the great fundamental principle of the law, ואהבת לרעך כמוך, "Thou shalt love thy neighbor as thyself!" or as Hillel explains it, דעלך סני לחברך לא תעביר, "Whatever is hateful to Thee, do not perpetrate against thy neighbor," with the remarkable addition, "This is the whole law; all else is its commentary."

Selfishness, therefore, is not only one of the greatest sins, but is the prolific source of every species of human wickedness. There is not a vice or a crime in the whole calendar of human aberrations, that may not be traced back to it as its fountain-head. The man, who respects neither the property, nor the honor, nor the peace, nor the life of his neighbor—who insinuates himself into the tender family circle, and ruthlessly undermines the domestic peace and bliss of others, until the beautiful fabric of family happiness becomes a desolate ruin—does not such a man unscrupulously place his own profit and gain, his own satisfaction, the gratification of his own desires, above the prosperity, the peace and happiness of others?

One of the great characteristics of the present day is a lowness, a sordidness, a frigidness of thought and feeling. Men think meanly of their nature, and hence their conduct is selfish. We do not, indeed, see men in general given up to gross vices. We do not meet around us the ferocity or beastly licentiousness of the savage state. We find many marks of improvement, when we compare the present with earlier ages. But there is little elevation of sentiment. Comparatively few seem to be conscious of their high origin and destiny, their capacities of excellence, their relations to God, their interest in eternity.

Thanks to God, in the history of every age and nation, amidst the ravages of ambition and the mean aims of selfishness, there have broken forth nobler sentiments, and the evidences of a heavenly virtue. Every age has been illustrated by men, who bore themselves like men, who were animated "by the spirit of God," and vindicated the cause of humanity—men, who in circumstances of great trial, have adhered to moral and religious principle, to the cause of persecuted truth—who have trodden the fairest gifts of fortune and the world in the pursuit of duty. This is the greatest value of history, that it introduces us to persons of this illustrious order; and its noblest use is, by their examples to nourish in us a conviction, that elevated purity of motive and conduct is not a dream of fancy, but that it is placed within our reach, and is the very end of our being.

VIII.

"THE SPIRIT OF GOD IN MAN,"

A SERIES OF FOUR SERMONS,

DELIVERED AT

TEMPLE EMANU-EL.

2.

Sabbath, March 16th, 1872.

"Take to thyself Joshua, the son of Nun, a man in whom there is spirit." (Numbers xxvii. 18).

JOSHUA was animated by a spirit of wisdom, the spirit of God, and it was in virtue of this attribute that he was appointed as the leader of Israel's host, the successor of the great man, Moses. We have seen in our last meditation on this subject, that, opposed to this spirit of God in man, is the human spirit manifested in selfishness; that, prompted by this spirit of selfishness, every man is apt to regard himself as the centre of creation; but that it is his duty to overcome this spirit of selfishness in thought, word and action, by cultivating the spirit of God—that is, by ministering to the happiness and well-being of others.

Now, in order to discharge our duty in this respect, *in ample form*, it is not enough to blunt the sharpest points of selfishness, to moderate our self-love in some particular instances—for in this way no general result would be attained—we have to go farther, we must apply the axe to the root of the evil, by earnestly endeavoring to ascertain for ourselves the place and the claims to which we are entitled in the human world around us. And this process must not be conducted in a superficial way, by putting a modest estimate on our importance for the little circle, in which we live, but descending to the actual grade which we occupy in the universe.

The celebrated saying, attributed to Thales, "Know thyself!" has a wider application than that, in which it is generally construed. For in order to understand what we actually are, we must know others also. The knowledge of the few dozen people, with whom we have intercourse, and of the city in which we live, is certainly of primary importance. But we must not stop here. Let us calmly contemplate our vast, spacious globe with its millions of human beings; let us cast a retrospective glance into the past, and see what large multitudes have been swept away—each generation constituting the whole of mankind—as well as look into the illimitable future before us, and think how many generations will yet come after us;—the earth everywhere and at all times an open, never satiated grave, and, at the same time, everywhere and at all times teeming with new births and productions; let us reflect how much splendor and misery, how much wisdom and folly, how much virtue and vice, this earth has already borne and is yet destined to bear! And then turning our eye from this earth, which can by no means appear to us as an atom, and raising it to the hosts of stars above us, we reflect that all those innumerable orbs are immeasurably larger spheres of divine providence, the habitations of living and sentient beings; and still to our short-sighted vision they appear as infinitesimal particles floating in the immensity and infinitude of space! When we reflect that all these worlds count their existence by thousands of years, and will continue to exist for thousands of years, after our bodies will have mouldered to dust; and then, astounded, amazed and stupified by such a contemplation, we descend to ourselves and ask ourselves the question, "What am I, and how much am I, a single, frail and erring individual in connection with this vast, unutterably vast sphere of beings?"—Will not our wisdom thus discover a standard for our littleness? Will not our pride be forced to exclaim, "How insignificant I am compared with this infinitude!"—And this whole vast universe is taken in by God at a glance, and is ruled by His providence!

After such a contemplation could we still presume to consider ourselves a centre, around which the whole world revolves—still cherish a desire of drawing all else into our individual sphere, of rendering all else subservient to our selfish ends? Would it not be more natural and more rational to bow our head in deep humility, and pray, "Father, I renounce my self-will, I wholly confide myself to Thee, to guide me in Thy wisdom, to assign me to the place I am fitted for, to aid me in applying the powers and means, with which Thou hast endowed me, to the welfare and happiness of Thy children."

In thus tearing the roots of selfishness from our bosom and subordinating our will to the will of God, we give evidence of being truly animated by the spirit of God.

But the work is to be done thoroughly. No bargaining, no set-offs, no subterfuges, no cunning devices must be resorted to. תמים תהיה עם ה' אלהיך. Complete as we are, with our plans and our wishes, our hopes and our fears, our predilections and our aversions, our strong and our weak points, undivided and without reserve, we must confide in and defer to God, if we mean to obey the promptings of the spirit of God within us. *The spirit of God within us*—for the heavenly voice, whose warnings and behests are constantly addressed to us, is within our own heart. אכן רוח היא באנוש ונשמת שדי תבינם "Truly, says Job, there is a spirit in man, and the breath of the Almighty giveth them understanding." And it is precisely this spirit, which spontaneously teaches every man, in every grade and condition, how utterly insignificent, how utterly worthless he would be, if isolated from the rest of his kind, if exclusively bound up in his own selfish individuality.

There are, indeed, many situations and occurrences in life, in which the feeling of our dependence is brought home to us with a crushing weight.

We may array ourselves in the most costly attire, with gems and jewels sparkling in brilliant profusion around our persons, still it is not only God who knows and sees, what Abraham expressed in sincere humility, "that we are but dust and ashes"—but we shall feel it ourselves, at times most inconvenient and unseasonable.

We may fancy ourselves to possess the highest culture, the most refined taste, the most penetrating understanding, still there are moments, in which we are forced to confess that our counsel is at fault, that all our wisdom is of no avail.

We may heap treasures of gold mountain high, "join house on house, bring field near to field, till there is no more room,"—still with all our wealth we are not able to purchase exemption from sickness, to secure perennial health.

We may command a host of servants, ministering to our comfort, attending to our wants, enabling us to pass a life of languid ease, of luxurious indolence—still we shall be compelled to undergo some indispensable personal exertion.

And who does not know, although he may seldom think of it, that one day, sooner or later, each one of us must meet the awful change, must submit to the universal law, from which even a Moses was not exempt, which consigns all that is mortal to decay and to death, and which summons his immortal soul to the bar of eternity! And as neither ornate finery nor wealth, neither accomplishments nor culture, neither rank nor station, can save us from this impending doom, these things will, in like manner, neither precede nor follow us to our eternal home, in order to plead for us, to assert there our claims to distinction and superiority.

But there is something which will precede us, which will plead our cause with imperishable eloquence and power. והלך לפניך צדקך, "Thy righteousness will go before thee." The good deeds which thou hast performed, will testify in thy favor to all eternity. And these good deeds, in order to be genuine, must flow from the spirit of God within us.

There are many deeds performed by man which are but specious counterfeits of real goodness, hypocritical devices to cover up actual moral obliquity. Who of you does not call to mind the occasional munificent charities of a once all-powerful, but now spotted and degraded politician of this city, paraded before the public eye with all the dazzling splendor of immaculate goodness and righteousness. Were not these charities the wages of corruption, designed to promote the selfish ends of their author? It argues well for human nature to look upon the *effect* and not upon the *motive* of deeds of charity. But when the crafty hypocrite stands unmasked before us in all the hideousness of his unrighteous, selfish manipulations, his charities are without intrinsic value, and can only serve "to point out a moral and adorn a—sermon." Charity of this kind is aptly compared in the Talmud טובל ושרץ בידו to a man, who performs the levitical ablution, while persistently grasping the unclean reptile, by which he was defiled.

The only true standard, by which our good deeds can be gauged, is the absence of selfishness. In looking around and above us with an intelligent eye, we must become aware of our individual insignificance, and that we are by no means the centre, around which the whole world revolves; we must gain the conviction that we are but satellites of the only great centre, around which all worlds and all created beings are revolving. And this great centre is God, whose spirit animates our being. Let us listen to the voice of this spirit within us, and our duties will be faithfully discharged, our task upon earth be accomplished for our own good and the happiness of others.

IX.

"THE SPIRIT OF GOD IN MAN,"

A SERIES OF FOUR SERMONS,

DELIVERED AT

TEMPLE EMANU-EL.

3.

Sabbath, March 30th, 1872.

Take to thyself Joshua, the Son of Nun, a man in whom there is spirit. (Numbers xxvii, 18).

IN my last two expositions of this text, I have endeavored to define the term רוח or spirit, the possession of which qualified Joshua, in an eminent degree, to succeed his great master as leader of the people, to marshal their hosts for the occupation of the promised land. I have tried to show, that every man is endowed with this spirit of God, to whose voice he must listen, in order to overcome the spirit of selfishness, which is lurking in the human heart; I have endeavored, to expose the fallacy of the wide-spread phenomenon, according to which every man is apt, to regard himself as the centre, around which the whole world is revolving; and have drawn the irresistible conclusion, that only those deeds, which are devoid of selfish motives and ends are emanations of the spirit of God within us, are entitled to be characterized as good and noble.

It is owing to the prevalence of the spirit of selfishness, that we meet with so little elevation of sentiment, and that comparatively few seem to be conscious of their high origin and destiny, their capacities of excellence, their relation to God, their interest in eternity.

The spirit of God, which is operative in man and by the prompting of which all that is good, great and noble is accomplished, the spirit of philanthropy and love, is confined to neither age, country or people, but is active, though in a limited degree and in isolated instances, at all times and in every place. Judaism does not favor pessimism; it abhors the idea of general depravity or original sin, but emphaticaly teaches the God-like character of the human soul. Hence we are justified in assuming, that the spirit of God is revealed and is manifested through man, just as much in our day, as at any previous period of history. We easily recognize this spirit by its *reverse*. Every manifestation or action, which excludes selfishness, is the product of this spirit; but wherever selfishness predominates, you look in vain for this spirit, for it is wanting.

Let us illustrate this proposition by a few examples.

The spirit of God is called the spirit of wisdom. What is wisdom? It is the choice of laudable ends and of the best means to accomplish them. Its scope is not limited to the individual, but embraces the welfare of the whole; is not bounded by our temporal existence, but includes time and eternity. While estimating material advantages and possessions at their comparative value, it is the chief aim of wisdom, to promote the intellectual and moral growth of mankind, its end the foundation of general good. The spirit of wisdom is essentially the spirit of benevolence.

Now contrast with this spirit of wisdom, the spirit of *worldly prudence*, by which most people are animated and which they apply to practice—a spirit which sternly asserts individual claims and rigidly aims at securing selfish ends—and you will no longer be at a loss, to discern the spirit of God, that should be reflected in our works. The prudent man may be just and moral, and yet be far from being benevolent and religious.

Justice differs from benevolence, not in its nature, but in the circumstances, under which it is exercised. Both justice and benevolence have the same object, the general good; but justice is limited to those cases where public good prescribes a clear, precise and unchanging course of action; while benevolence or its daughter—mercy, is exercised in circumstances, to which no definite rules can be applied, and in which the general good requires, that the individual should be left to his own judgment and discretion. Thus true justice is something more than that petty honesty, which seeks nothing but self, and which is contented with regarding such established principles as cannot be violated without incurring punishment or disgrace. The whole nature of justice is *impartial, diffusive benevolence.*

It may be observed, that, if it be the nature of justice to avoid, whatever is clearly opposed to our neighbor, it is unjust, in our dealings with others, to desire and seek more than the value of our services and commodities. Mutual benefit is the object of all human relations, the very end of trade or commerce. We know, when our neighbor contracts with us, that he expects an equivalent. We know, that he renders his services, or makes a transfer of his property for some adequate valuable consideration, and we have no right to offer as an equivalent, what we certainly know bears no proportion to the services he renders or the property he transfers. A just man, animated by the spirit of God, will never lose sight of the interests of his neighbor. He will not, indeed, feel himself bound, to take the same care of another's property and interests as of his own—for this is impracticable. He will suppose, that every man, who possesses common understanding, knows best his own interests, and on this ground he will deal with him. But when he certainly knows, that his neighbor is injuring himself, that a proposed contract cannot be attended with mutual benefit, he has no right to presume that his neighbor is taking care of himself; he has no right to be determined upon realizing the fruits of his shrewd and sharp transaction. As surely as he regards the rights of others, he will feel, that he has no right to offer as an equivalent, what he knows has no proportionate value.

Yes, it is but too true, that justice unconnected with benevolence is not worth possessing. It is the growth of selfishness, and knaves may boast of it. That man, who makes his own private interest supreme—who monopolises all honors, emoluments and profits that appertain to his province—who cares not how much his neighbor suffers, if only his individual interests be advanced, —who can take pleasure in gains which, he knows, are necessarily connected with the loss and injury of others— who, under pretence of leaving his neighbor to provide for himself, will impose upon him as an equivalent, what he knows to be worth nothing : that man may talk of integrity, and hold high his head in a prudent, mercenary world, but he knows not the meaning of justice. He never felt that *generous* regard to right, that noble appreciation of religion and benevolence, which is of more worth and confers more happiness than all the gains of selfishness.

If such be perfect justice, so incorruptible, what reason have we to fear, that there is little of this principle, when we see the expedients and precautions, which are adopted to prevent men from abusing a trifling or important trust, from sacrificing the interests of their neighbor to a trifling or important gain! We carry our own shame on our

own foreheads. Most of our civil institutions grow out
of our corruptions and delinquencies. We cannot live
without mutual dependence, and yet we are forced, to
hedge each other round, to bind and shackle each other,
to institute inquiries and to watch with anxious caution,
less we should abuse each other's necessities, and take
advantage of trust, to betray it. At this very moment,
here and elsewhere throughout the country, in the General, the State and Municipal government, active investigations are carried on, to ascertain, to what an extent
the public functionaries have betrayed the various trusts
confided to them. Yes, is it not suggestive, is it not
humiliating, that a necessity existed for the appointment
of a "Committee on Frauds?"—If men were, what they
should be, if all were animated by the true spirit, we should
find in every man a guardian, instead of an invader of
our rights and interests. We should want no better security than our neighbor's word, and no better witness
than our neighbor's conscience. Imagination dwells
with delight on this state of peaceful, unsuspicious, undisturbed enjoyment. Is it never to be made a reality?
Will the era never dawn on the horizon of man, of which
the prophet speaks, לא ירעו ולו ישחיתו בכל הר קדשי, "They
shall do no hurt nor destroy in all my holy mountain,
saith the Lord—?"

It is the glorious design of civil institutions to concentre public strength in support of individual right, to
guard the interests of the feeble by the majesty of the
State. But no government can fully accomplish the end
of its institution. No outward penalties can supply the
place of an inward principle of benevolence, of genuine
religion. They, who have power, can always find some
opportunity of abusing it. Judaism, the exponent of
true religion, an emanation from God, emphatically
holds, האומר שלי שלי ושלך שלך זו מדת סדום "whoever saith:

What is mine, is mine; and what is thine, is thine; pronounces a doctrine of Sodom." True religion forbids us, to abuse any circumstance, which puts our neighbor in our power, or to extort his consent to injurious measures, or to reduce him to the necessity of sacrificing his property, by threatening him with evils, to which we are able to expose him. It recommends the weak and poor to our protection. It renders the defenceless hovel of poverty as sacred as the palace of affluence. It makes the cause of the oppressed our own, and animates us with generous zeal, to rescue the helpless from the grasp of the oppressor. It calls on us, to frown on the base, to separate ourselves from their fellowship הרחק משכן רע to keep none of their counsels, to follow none of their examples. Men are prone to stoop to successful villany. They seem to forget the steps, by which wicked men have ascended to eminence. They have only eyes for the outward splendor and seeming prosperity, in which successful villany is revelling. But the spirit of God within man is inflexible. It can give no countenance to dishonesty and wrong. It looks through the false splendor, with which the selfish are surrounded, and sees and detests their baseness.

A man animated by this spirit takes a firm, elevated ground. He does not cling to every shadow of right. He does not take advantage of ambiguity of expression, to beat down what he knows to be a substantial claim. He does not abuse the ignorance of his neighbor and uphold, by legal subleties, an unfounded demand. He does not press even his undoubted rights too close, lest he should border upon injustice. He reverences the laws, as they are the guardians of right. He holds nothing merely because the laws do not take it away. He seizes nothing merely because the laws do not prohibit it. His motto is not: I will take all the law allows me. He considers, that laws do not create right, that there are eternal principles of truth and rectitude, to which all civil laws must be reduced as their standard; and to the spirit planted by God in the human heart and revealed in His holy word, he refers all his actions, which relate to his dealings and his intercourse with others.

There is a natural law, that whatever belongs to the earth, presses towards its centre. You may pick up a stone, and fling it high in the air—it is sure to fall back to the ground, from which is was taken. A mysterious force in the dark bosom of the earth irresistibly draws it down, as it attracts every object and every particle, that belongs to the earth. In a similar way does *selfishness* act in man. It is the power of *gravitation* in the human heart, a power, which, if left uncontrolled, would fain attract to its centre all *earthly* objects, means and appliances and hold them fast with iron bands. Selfishness is thus synonymous with darkness of soul, frigidity of heart, spiritual death.

But there is another law of nature, which governs the operations of *light*. Its power is not exerted in drawing all things to its centre, but is, on the contrary, manifested, by shedding its rays, and pouring its warmth on all objects within its reach. This power preeminently, exclusively resides in the spirit of God within man. It is manifested in our diffusing the light of knowledge, in our pouring forth the warming rays of sympathy, of virtue, of benevolence, of true religion. It does not contract, but expands the heart, inuring it to all that is good, and true, and noble, and divine. O, that such a light would burn in every heart. "Would to God, that the whole people were prophets, that the Lord would endow them with His spirit."

X.

"THE SPIRIT OF GOD IN MAN,"

A SERIES OF FOUR SERMONS,

DELIVERED AT

TEMPLE EMANU-EL.

4.

Sabbath, April 13th, 1872.

" Take unto thyself Joshua, the son of Nun, a man in whom there is spirit." (Numbers xxvii., 18.)

THESE words, which thrice constituted the basis of our meditation, force themselves upon our particular attention to-day, by the Haphtarah, which has been read to us, how Joshua, a man in whom there was spirit, the true spirit of God, prepared himself for the last hour.

After a long career of victorious warfare, followed by an old age of comparative repose, during which, upon his estate at Timnath Serach, in the mountains of Ephraim, he was permitted to enjoy the blessings of the land he had conquered, Joshua consciously drew nigh to the term of his existence and, like Moses, determined to give to the assembled Israelites the advantage of his parting counsels. The tribes were convened at Shechem, where the Tabernacle at this time seems to have been, and where, on a former occasion, between the mountains of Ebal and Gerizzim, they had entered into covenant with God. Nothing can be conceived, more impressive or sublime, than the circumstance of this last public interview of the aged leader with the people, whom he had put in possession of the goodly promised land, and who had so often followed him in his victorious path. In the midst of the elders, the chiefs, and magistrates of Israel, surrounded by a respectful people, their illustrious and venerable commander—the oldest man in the nation—spoke to them as to his sons. And of what did he speak? He was a soldier, and his career had been essentially military; but he spoke to them, not of conquest—the sound of the trumpet and the gleam of the sword cannot be recognized in his address—but of the holiness and the obedience which became the people of God. It is such a discourse as a patriarch might have given on his death-bed, or a prophet might have uttered from the valley of the vision. There is nothing like it in modern history, except the prophetic and inspired Farewell Address of our immortal Washington.

He called to mind the benefits, which, age after age, had been showered upon the race of Abraham; he humbly summed up the victories to which he had himself led them, in a single allusion; and concluded, with the impressive words, "Choose ye, this day, whom ye will serve; but as for me and my house, we will serve the Lord." The entire people, with one voice, responded to this call by loud and hearty declarations of their determined faithfulness to their covenant with God. And the aged Joshua, after he had written these words in the book of the law, deposited in the ark, set up a stone under a tree that grew near the Tabernacle, as a memorial of the renewal of the covenant. His work, both of war and of peace, was then done. He could now lay down his head and die in thankful peace.

My friends, whoever can act, whoever can speak thus in the last hours of his earthly career, must have lived a life, in accordance with the promptings of the "spirit of God" within him. No fear, no misgiving, no terror, can shake his equanimity. With a serene calm, with a settled composure, with a holy peace, he bids adieu to the world; and the more rationally he may have loved the world, the more tenderly he may have been attached to his fellow-men, the more calmly he will depart.

The *world!*—What is comprehended in this term?— In its current application, the world is employed to designate the goods and pleasures of the earth, in so far as they gratify the senses more than the *spirit.* Whoever finds delight in the goods and pleasures of the earth, and strives to obtain the first, and to enjoy the last—of him we say, that he loves the world.

Is it our duty, or is it a sin, to love the world?—In former times there were many people, who withdrew from the world, and retired into solitude—from *piety.* They *hated* the world, scornfully spurned its goods, and disdained its pleasures. It would be difficult, to find a satisfactory answer to the question: What did these people want upon earth—what did they wish to accomplish for the good of mankind? As far as Judaism is concerned, neither the Mosaic nor the prophetical books, neither the Talmud nor any rabbinical writings, attach the least merit, the least religious value, to a withdrawal from the active scenes of life. Judaism, on the contrary, insists upon an active intermingling with the world, to develop our powers and faculties for our own good, and for the benefit of our fellow-men. It is opposed to a sanctimonious, morose, misanthropical view of life. It recommends cheerfulness. It says, עבדו את ה' בשמחה "Serve ye the Lord with joy!" אין השכינה שורה אלא מתוך שמחה. "The spirit of God only abides in a cheerful heart." It does not denounce the love of the world, provided our aspirations and indulgences are kept within *reasonable,* within *rational* bounds.

For whom can the earth have its treasures, and the world its joys? For whom is nature renewed in her smiling vernal attire? For whom do the trees yield their fruit—the olive its fatness—the vine its juice? 'Is it to rejoice the beasts of the field? 'No, no, you may love the world—but you shall love it rationally, appreciate it correctly, and indulge in wise moderation. And this you are sure to do, when you consider, that the treasures and joys of the world are gifts of God and, hence, are designed to subserve wise and good purposes. There is no absolute evil. Even the *poisons* in nature are good in themselves. Wisely chosen, compounded and administered by the skilful physician, they produce a salutary effect. Injudiciously used, they kill, instead of preserving life. And that is precisely the case with the treasures and pleasures of the world. You may strive for possession with prudent care, with wise discretion; you may indulge with rational moderation: the possession will thus be meritorious and laudable—the enjoyments have a salutary effect. Such is the language of Judaism, such is the language of reason.

And it says further: The world, with all its treasures, its pleasures and its glories, will pass away. No earthly good endures, no earthly joy is lasting—only the gains and joys of the spirit will endure forever. Whatever of an earthly nature we possess or enjoy, is subject to change and decay. גלגול חוזר בעולם. Ask your own experience. Many a one entered the arena of life, under the bright rays of a glorious morning sun, but before he had yet reached noon, the horizon was covered with thick clouds, and the sky became dark and gloomy. Many a tender babe, tenderly nursed by delicate hands, surrounded by luxury, pampered by indulgence the most exquisite—but a few short years had passed, when the boy or the maiden was exposed to pinching want, because fortune, in her fickleness, had turned her back upon the parents, and surrendered the children to the rough usage, to the cold charities of the world. Who, therefore, does not perceive the instability, the precarious tenure, by which we hold and enjoy all that is earthly, and appreciate the world according to its true value? Who would build upon sand, when he can chose a firm, solid foundation?

Judaism further says—in full harmony with reason — Since all the possessions and enjoyments of life come from God, you may wisely enjoy them, and render thanks to God. ואכלת ושבעת וברכת את ה' אלהיך. But in what way can we best express our gratitude to God? Is it by thanks, couched in words of prayer? Is the offering of grace, before or after meal, sufficient acknowledgment for the abundance, with which God has blessed us? Prayer, it is true, is a gratifying, a salutary exercise, most natural to the man endowed with the spirit of God. In prayer, we become more fully conscious of the grateful thoughts and feelings, which animate our bosom. Prayer, therefore, should constitute a regular, sacred family practice in every Jewish home. But our gratitude to God for the blessings we enjoy is not to be limited to fine sentiments, nor to beautifully turned words. It finds its true expression in deeds. When we console the afflicted; when we dry the tears of the unfortunate; when we soothe the wounds of hearts lacerated by grief; when we feed the hungry, clothe the naked, relieve the oppressed; when we aid and support, whenever our aid and support can sustain the tottering and falling; when we distribute from our abundance, to chase away the ghastly spectres of want and misery from the fireside of the poor—then, and then only, do we express genuine gratitude to God for the blessings we enjoy. We cease to be men, and become ministering angels on God's beautiful earth. Our earthly treasures cease to be dross and sordid pelf, but are transformed into treasures of heaven, because they enable us to perform God-like offices upon earth.

Active benevolence and charity is one of those virtues, of which, the Mishnah says, we enjoy the fruits in this life, while the principal remains unimpaired for the life hereafter. The Jubilee of charity, celebrated a few evenings ago, affords a practical illustration of this doctrine. Whose heart was not touched by genuine satisfaction, was not filled with a holy joy, on reflecting, that hundreds of helpless, innocent orphans, are tenderly cared for, and prepared for the battle of life by the provident hand of charity? It was, indeed, enjoying the fruit of your benefaction. The words cheerily sung forth by the shrill voices of your beneficiaries could not but have impressed themselves upon the assembled multitude:—

> Where the shelterless
> Standeth comfortless,
> Let thine eye in loving kindness turn;
> To the motherless,
> Ne'er be pitiless—
> Let thy heart and hand with blessings burn;
> Through the wilderness,
> Streams of tenderness
> Pour from out thy fountain's full supply;
> All the wretchedness
> Turn to blessedness,
> So shalt thou receive reward on high.

No, no, the idea of parting with the world, its possessions and its pleasures, never causes disquietude to him, who has estimated them at their true value. The enjoyments of earth have not rendered him a slave, the possession of its treasures have not exclusively engrossed his heart. He has tasted, in wise moderation, the one and made a rational use of the other. This conviction stands at his side, like an angel of light, breathing comfort, peace and hope into the soul, when soaring aloft to the regions of immortality.

XI.

ORATION

Delivered at the Laying of the Corner-Stone

OF THE

HOME FOR JEWISH· WIDOWS AND ORPHANS

OF NEW ORLEANS,

August 7th, 1855.

LADIES AND GENTLEMEN:—A solemn and interesting ceremony has been performed; the cornerstone of an edifice devoted to the objects of charity and benevolence has been laid. The superstructure to be raised on this foundation will be a noble monument to the undying generous impulses of humanity that prompted this sacred enterprise; to the unflagging zeal which hastened it to a successful issue. We have assembled to celebrate the triumph of philanthropy over selfishness; of active benevolence over grasping avarice; of diffusive sympathy with the condition of our fellow-beings over callous and soul-cramping indifference. Works like this are calculated to redeem the character of our age, and bespeak for it the veneration and regard of succeeding generations. Works like this bear testimony that material tendencies, immoderate love of lucre and flinty selfishness do not form the exclusive characteristics of our community; but that the founders of this institution are fully alive to the claims of humanity, and are ready, to the extent of their power, to alleviate the sufferings and lighten the burden of distress, by which they are surrounded.

However numerous the benevolent institutions of our city may be, however various their objects, and however liberally supported, still a serious void has been most sensibly felt for some time past. By degrees the desideratum, at first but casually hinted at, aroused a general and most lively interest—a noble enthusiasm fanned the glimmering sparks into a bright burning flame —the scattered forces assembled in public meeting— diverging sentiments and views were made to harmonize —a well-digested plan was adopted—an association organized and incorporated—and, thanks to the well-directed efforts of the energetic President and his no less energetic coadjutors, the Board of Directors of the Association—thanks to the willing sacrifices of the community at large, we have this day had the gratification of laying the corner-stone of "The Home for Jewish Widows and Orphans of New Orleans."

There is nothing in which the moderns claim more conspicuously to surpass the ancients than in the noble provisions for the relief of indigence and distress. The public policy of the ancients seems to have embraced only whatever might promote the aggrandizement or the direct prosperity of the State, and to have cared little for those unfortunate beings who, from poverty or incapacity of any kind, were disqualified from contributing to this. Their cultivation of the fine arts may be said in the language of their own poet,

"Ingenuas didicisse fideliter artes,
Emollit mores, nec sinit esse feros,"

to have softened their manners, and to have reclaimed them from barbarity; yet that beautiful line, *Homo sum*, *nil humani a me alienum puto!* "I am a man and deem myself affected by whatever pertains to humanity"— although greeted with one spontaneous burst of applause by the assembled multitude, appears to have been admired as a fine sentiment, but failed to be recognized as a rule of action in the varied interests and wants of society But the beneficent influence of Scriptural ethics, combined with the general tendency of our social institutions, has led to the recognition of rights in the individual as sacred as those of the community, and has suggested manifold provisions for personal comfort and happiness. The spirit of benevolence and philanthropy is coeval with the origin of the Bible. The Law, the Prophets and the Sacred Writings enforce it on their every page. The more widely and sincerely, therefore, the authority of the Bible is acknowledged, the more generally will this noble spirit be diffused, softening the asperities of life, and mitigating the evils and adversities that grow out of the peculiar condition and inequalities of the social state. The spirit of benevolence and kindness is of origin divine; yet to the credit and honor of human nature be it said, that in its most general and comprehensive sense, we designate it by the name of HUMANITY.

I have said that the spirit of benevolence and philanthropy is coeval with the origin of the Bible. A mere glance at its contents will prove the correctness of this proposition. It is remarkable, indeed, that centuries before the renowned bard of Hellas sang in inimitable lines the warlike achievements, heroic adventures and primitive habits of his age—centuries before Genius, under the fancied inspiration of the muses, displayed its versatile powers in the production of those poetical and plastic creations, which form the pride of heathen antiquity and constitute models of taste for succeeding ages

—centuries before the liberal arts *did* "soften the manners of man and reclaim him from barbarity," the Mosaic polity had already enunciated those sublime doctrines of faith, which in the end will be universally adopted, and established those principles of morality, which form the only correct standard of all true civilization, and really tend to humanize mankind. Under this system the mind became enlarged under the awful contemplation of the One, the Father of the Universe, and the heart became expanded with the sentiments of true philanthropy, that formed the basis of the Divine code of laws. It would be improper on this occasion to dilate on the principles of justice, liberty and equality that characterize all its provisions, but the spirit of its charitable institutions and enactments well deserves a brief notice at our hands.

The public institutions for the relief of the poor and needy, under the Mosaic system, were in keeping with the usages of that remote age and the occupation of the people—agriculture being the principal pursuit. They consisted in tithes and gleanings from the field, the orchard and the vineyard. But from the benefit of these charitable provisions none was excluded. The stranger in the gates had an equal claim with the native born Israelite to this harvest of the poor. It was intended for the afflicted, the needy, the stranger, the widow and the orphan, that all might enjoy the blessings of God.

In like manner does Scripture enjoin the dispensation of private charity, on the broad principle of comprehensive benevolence. "If thy brother become poor, and fall in decay with thee, then shalt thou assist him, a stranger, or a sojourner, that he may live with thee." "If there be among thee a needy man of one of thy brethren, within any of thy gates, thou shalt not harden thy heart, nor shut thy hand from thy needy brother:

thou shalt open wide thy hand unto thy brother, to thy poor and to thy needy in the land." Particular stress is laid on the support and aid to be granted to the widow and the fatherless, and the neglect of this duty was accounted one of the most grievous sins. Job, in reviewing his past life, pathetically exclaims in self-justification, "Have I ever denied the wish of the poor, or have I allowed the eyes of the widow to fail in vain hope? Have I ever eaten my bread by myself alone, and the fatherless did not eat thereof? Yea, I delivered the poor that cried, and the fatherless, that had none to help him; the blessing of him that was ready to perish came upon me, and the heart of the widow I caused to sing for joy."

This spirit of charity and benevolence, instilled by law and precept, celebrated in the glowing language of the inspired writers, and strengthened by practice, forever remained the distinguishing characteristic of the people of the Bible. For a long time exposed to the scorn, the contumely and persecution of the world, the Israelites practically demonstrated this spirit of charity and benevolence, in magnanimously forgiving and forgetting untold injuries and wrongs; in extending the hand of brotherhood to the reconciled foe; in supporting the needy of his kindred and faith; in sympathizing deeply with human suffering; in being ever prompt to afford relief; in assisting in the promotion of every scheme tending to enhance the improvement and increase the happiness of our common race.

> "Where'er we roamed—along the brink
> Of Rhine, or by the sweeping Po,
> Through Alpine vale or champaign wide,
> Whate'er we looked on, at our side
> Was Charity—to bid us think
> And feel, and kindness show."

And these principles we still cherish—and this spirit we still foster, with a devotion that shrinks from no obstacle and is ever sanguine of success. The cause of philanthropy addresses itself to the noblest impulses of the human heart. Wherever it flourishes, there is true civilization. Here, in the land of the free and the home of the brave, it finds a genial soil; for the free are generous, and the brave humane. Under the glorious banner of our blessed country we may freely pursue our mission of peace, and found institutions for the promotion of the comfort and well-being of our suffering fellow-creatures. As the broad sheet of "the Father of Waters" glides in its majestic grandeur along this bank, bearing on its bosom manifold products of God's blessing and man's industry: thus may our charity expand and in its course supply the wants of the needy and minister to the comforts of the poor, console the widow and protect the orphan.

Of all the Jewish congregations that are now existing in this country, or that are in the progress of formation, there is not one that had not its origin in the organization of a benevolent society, or to which from its very beginning some charitable institution had not been attached. And these benevolent associations are not founded upon the principle of mutual relief societies, whose benefits are confined to their own members. Their objects are purely charitable. Their members enjoy no other privilege but that of dispensing with prudence and circumspection the aggregate sum of their own annual dues and voluntary contributions in a manner best fitted to promote the general good. And it is mainly owing to this systematic charity, or rather charitable system, that few, if any, of the descendants of Abraham are found among the inmates of the public charities. The solicitude manifested on our part to save our co-religionists from becoming dependent on a public charity, is not so much founded in religious considerations, as in the conviction that the chief object of charity is to prevent pauperism. This object, however, can only be accomplished by tendering our aid to the poor, while he has yet the strength to retrieve his broken fortunes, while the consciousness of his dignity and the hope of a better future have not yet departed from his bosom.

For the last eleven years the Hebrew Benevolent Association has been in active operation. Before yet a Synagogue was built, this society had been instituted and incorporated. Its object is to grant relief to the poor and sick of the Jewish persuasion in this city and its vicinity. Generously has it been supported, and nobly has it performed its mission. Many a poor stranger, fleeing from the tyranny and oppression of European governments and seeking an asylum on these hospitable shores, has received its timely succor and been provided with the means to gain an honest living. And there are instances on record of individuals thus relieved gratefully refunding the amount granted to them, and becoming active members of an institution, to whose well-timed assistance, they were indebted for their independence. The home of many a poor family has been rendered cheerful by the dropping of its bounty; and many a poor pilgrim, stricken down with disease far from his home and kindred, has received at its hands that aid and sympathy which, under Providence, snatched him from the portals of death, or, at least, soothed the last solemn hours of his life.

During the ever-memorable epidemic season of 1853, near 4,500 dollars were expended by this Association for the relief of the sick and poor, and I may safely aver, that during the comparatively short period of its existence more than $30,000 have been disbursed by it for charitable objects.

For several years this association stood alone in the field of benevolence. But, as with the increase of our population the calls for relief became more numerous and varied, a new and powerful ally made its appearence. In 1847, the Hebrew Ladies' Benevolent Society was organized. Need I speak of the zeal and devotion with which this society entered the lists to combat the ills of life to which the poor and destitute are exposed ? As well might I attempt to praise the beaming moon in a cloudless night for the soothing light of her silver rays, or the rose for the sweetness of its fragrance. Who is not aware of the deep, abiding affections that dwell in the heart of woman !- In her gentle nature she is the living representative of charity. Her warm sympathy is ever sure to soothe the afflicted and to comfort the broken-hearted ; for " the law of kindness is on her tongue. " She lends to prosperity its transcendent lustre, and inspires adversity with fortitude, resignation and hope. And whilst her eye is melting with the tear of compassion, " she spreadeth out wide her hand to the poor ; yea, her hands she stretcheth forth to the needy." Well may we say, with the sage of old, " Give her of the fruit of her hands, and let her own works praise her in the gates. "

Another society of two years standing is " The Hebrew Foreign Mission. " As the title indicates, it has for its object the amelioration of the spiritual, social and political condition of Israelites in foreign countries. But it is likewise within its province to introduce a system of colonization, with a special view to the creating of settlements in this country, in which the peaceful habits of agricultural and pastoral life, to which the people of Israel was exclusively devoted in the days of old, may be re-established. As yet this society is in its infancy, and has produced no practical effect. But who can doubt its future beneficial results ? who cannot foresee that in the end it will be subsidiary, to some extent, in developing the resources and raising the moral influence of our country ?

Another important charitable institution of recent date owes its origin to the munificence of one man. It commemorates a name that will ever be dear to us, will ever be honored by the good and benevolent, and be specially blessed by those who shall reap the benefits of that institution. I refer to the Jewish Hospital, known under the name of the Touro Infirmary, the bequest of our late lamented fellow-citizen Judah Touro. Its objects and necessity are easily comprehended. For although the Charity Hospital, a State institution, and the noble Howards, a band of disinterested, high-minded citizens, have the specific object of extending their aid to all who may require it—although the Hebrew Benevolent Association has devoted its best energies to the relief of the poor and homeless in times of sicksess and desolation : yet the expediency of a Hospital, where patients, whose religious convictions and profoundest hopes are in unison with ours, receive the requisite attention and treatment under our own supervision, will be admitted by every well-disposed mind. Thrice blessed be the memory of that good old man, whose last acts were in keeping with the eminently benevolent tenor of his whole life—whose philanthropy was unprejudiced—whose charity, although judiciously beginning at home, was yet not restricted to the pale of his own creed, but exceeded the boundaries of the latter, and extended its benefits even to distant communities.

In the course of my remarks I have given a succinct history of our Jewish benevolent institutions. Each of them has a laudable object, and demonstrated the necessity of its existence. Whoever is acquainted with the details of their operations must have observed their usefulness and the happy results attained through their agency. But it cannot be overlooked that the relief granted by the above-mentioned charities is only of a temporary character ; and yet there is a class of unfortunate beings among us who, from the helplessness of their condition, demand our permanent support and protection. The poor widow who mourns the loss of a beloved husband, to whom she clung in prosperity and adversity, in weal and woe, at whose side she was contented in the humblest station, and resigned to the severest strokes of fortune ; the orphan who is deprived of his natural protectors, and forever remains a stranger to the sweet influences of home, that exert their power and are remembered with a melting tenderness to the last day of life ; the one with the finer sensibilities of her sex and the contracted sphere of her resources cramped in her exertion to secure a maintenance ; the other with powers and capacities yet undeveloped, tossed about by the fierce waves of privation, and hunger, and unguided impulse—these unfortunate beings, every one must admit, cannot be left to the temporary relief of a charitable society or to the caprice and chance of private benevolence, without jeopardizing their very existence.

An eminent modern writer thus graphically depicts the precarious condition of the fatherless. "There seems, " he says, "to be a sort of chance in the lot of the orphan offspring of the poor. On some the eye of benevolence falls at the very first moment of their uttermost destitution—and their worst sorrows, instead of beginning, terminate with the tears shed over their parents, graves. They are taken by the hand, as soon as their hands have been stretched out for protection, and admitted as inmates into households, whose doors, had their fathers and mothers been alive, they would never have darkened.. The light of comfort falls upon them during the gloom of grief, and attends them all their days. Others, again, are overlooked at the first fall of affliction, as if by some unaccountable fatality ; the wretchedness, with which all have become familiar, no one very tenderly pities ; and thus the orphan, reconciling herself to the extreme hardships of her condition, lives on uncheered by those sympathies out of which grow both happiness and virtue, and yielding by degrees to the constant pressure of her lot, remains poor in spirit as in estate, and either vegetates like an almost worthless weed, that is carelessly trodden on by every foot, or if by nature born a flower, in time loses her lustre, and all the days leads the life of wretchedness and misery."

To preclude the possibility of so gloomy a lot ; to provide a home for the homeless ; to offer a retreat to the venerable matron and solace her widowed heart in her declining age ; to come to her assistance, when in the loneliness of her grief and the intensity of her affliction she lifts up her weeping eyes on high, exclaiming, "O Father, whence shall come my help ?" to relieve her mind from the sordid cares, paltry wants and petty humiliations, that would shroud her weak timid nature in the gloom of despair ; to provide an asylum for the fatherless ; to watch over the tender years of their childhood with a mother's affection ; to superintend their bodily wants and promote their mental culture ; to guard them from temptation and vice ; to elicit the faculties of their minds and teach them the ways of religion, of virtue, of honor and of rectitude ; to equip them for life's perilous voyage, that they may become useful members of society, and feel that they too have a portion in God's beautiful heritage :—to realize these transcendently noble and philanthropic ends, this institution has been founded.

Shall I farther elaborate its objects ? No, I must forbear. It would be presuming too much on your indulgence, which I fear I have already overtaxed. Only this let me say in conclusion.

The institution which has this day been founded is the youngest and fairest of her Hebrew sister-charities, and deserves to become the cherished pet of our community. The zeal and devotion that have hitherto characterized your exertions in its behalf, must not be suffered to cool. Additional sacrifices, no doubt, will be required to place it on a firm and permanent basis, and to fully realize the purposes for which it was called into life. Let these sacrifices be promptly made when needed. Let the spirit of benevolence and philanthropy continue to guide your deliberations and labors, and the blessing of God will prosper your design. And as the eye is riveted by the soft light of the morning dawn, the heart by the chains of love, the mind by the power of truth—so may your generous impulses be directed, with an abiding solicitude, towards " The Home for Jewish Widows and Orphans of New Orleans. "

XII.

ORATION

Delivered on the Fifth Anniversary

OF THE

HOME FOR JEWISH WIDOWS AND ORPHANS

OF NEW ORLEANS,

January 8th, 1851.

THE sun of the glorious Eighth of January has again reached its meridian altitude. Shedding its rays upon those fields rendered memorable by patriotic valor, it warms our hearts with patriotic fervor, kindling anew the memories and associations which cluster around this day, and around " the good men and true," who staked their lives for their country's good. Forty-six years have elapsed since the last invader was met and vanquished upon American soil—upon Louisiana's sunny plains. From the date of that victory no foreign foe has dared approach our shores, or molest our flag. Secure in our conscious strength, our resources were steadily developing. All the elements constituting a nation's greatness were active in working out and clearly defining our country's proud destiny. Material prosperity, moral progress, social advancement, political growth, and all the attributes of an enlightened civilization and of an increasing powerful influence may be traced in the history of this short period, in a degree that is without parallel in the annals of mankind. The young Eagle, growing apace and soaring aloft, had his eye steadily fixed upon the great orb of liberty as the fountain of his strength and the condition of his life.

A day suggestive of such reflections is fit to be honored as the holiday of freemen. For, what mean the thundering voices of the booming cannon which greeted the shades of yesternight and broke upon our slumbers at this morning's early dawn? What mean those gallant bands of citizen-soldiery that parade our streets to the enlivening strains of martial melody? What mean those flags, which, from dome and mast, float upon the breeze? What mean all these indications of a general holiday, military and civic, public and private?—They are, surely, no preparations to repel a foreign foe; nor are they merely the signs of a vain popular enthusiasm, venting itself in hollow show and empty pageant. They have a deep significance. These jubilant demonstrations are to us unequivocal pledges that the spirit of the fathers has descended upon the sons; that, as in days gone by, the people rose as one man in defence of RIGHT, JUSTICE, and LIBERTY, they are ready to do so again, whenever and from whatever quarter the attempt should be made, to crush these precious legacies secured to us by solemn compact.

The occasion for which we have met within these walls, is in keeping with the historic character of the day. We celebrate the anniversary of the founding of an institution whose object it is, to do battle with and to overcome the misfortunes and distresses, to which a portion of our fellow creatures are subjected. We celebrate the triumph of philanthropy—a cause which brings into play the noblest instincts of human nature. If patriotism is the crown of the citizen, charity adorns the man.

Five years have elapsed since the Home for Jewish

Widows and Orphans was dedicated to its sacred purposes. During this period of its existence, not only its necessity and usefulness, but also the active sympathy and liberal support of our community in its behalf have been fully demonstrated. Whilst the original thirteen inmates, with whom it was opened, have swelled to the number of souls which Jacob brought down with him to Egypt, the number of contributing members and the amount of extraordinary donations have increased in proportion. We have the satisfaction of knowing that its bounties could be, and were, dispensed without stint or limitation. No test of nativity is contained in our Constitution and By-laws, nor is there an instance on our records, in which the board of officers had not acted in the most liberal spirit, in the consideration of any application presented to them. And thus not only natives of Louisiana, but also of our sister States, Alabama, Mississippi, Tennessee, South Carolina, Missouri, Ohio, and New York—and of foreign countries, of Poland, Germany, France, Belgium, Holland, England, the West Indies and Canada—have found shelter within our Home. If it be borne in mind, that with the exception of Mobile, where we have sixteen regular members, a few Southern States, in which some of our regular contributors are scattered, and the city appropriation, to which we are entitled by law, we receive no permanent appreciable support from any quarter, and that the deficiency in the large expenditure for the maintenance of our institution has to be covered, annually, by our own voluntary subscriptions, in addition to our annual dues—the liberality displayed in the granting of the benefits of our Home will become still more conspicuous. The past five years have shown both our capacity and our willingness to do good in the right direction. Our Home is no longer an experiment, but a fact. Its beneficial results are patent to all. Other communities have followed our example. The innocent babe yet unconscious of its forlorn state—the guileless child, tearfully looking about for some guiding, protecting hand—the helpless matron, yearning for some quiet place, where to repose her troubled head and heal the wounds of her afflicted heart, have alike enjoyed the protection, the fostering care and domestic comfort suitable to their age and condition, within the walls of our Home. The gratifying results, the amount of good thus far achieved, must engender within us the desire to increase and render permanent the efficiency of our institution—to place it beyond the contingency of a failure—to secure to it a perpetual basis—to create it into a monument "more enduring than bronze," bearing testimony to the children and the children's children of the charitable disposition and noble generosity of their fathers.

In what language, more impressive and more touching, can fathers speak to their children, than in the language of those noble monuments, which are speaking evidences of the pious and benevolent sentiments that animated their hearts? Whenever we cross the threshold of an institution devoted to the amelioration of suffering humanity or to the mental and moral improvement of our race, we are seized with emotions of the profoundest gratitude and reverence for the memory of its founder. We feel that we stand on holy ground. A sympathetic chord is touched in our hearts. We are forced to admire the palpable evidences of the nobler instincts which God has implanted in the human soul. The selfishness of our nature is hushed. Bright visions of philanthropy and love dawn upon our mind, and seldom we leave the consecrated spot without conceiving the firm resolve, to contribute our share to the furtherance of general good, to exercise the God-like privilege of protecting the weak, comforting the desolate, instructing the ignorant, and supporting the needy. The Girard College, the Astor Library, the Smithsonian Institute, the Touro Almshouse and Touro Infirmary, are enduring and honorable monuments to the memories of their respective founders. These and similar institutions speak in a language that is universally understood, the sound of which will be distinctly heard above the selfish clamor of the present and of future generations.

Is it not natural, then, that you should glory in the idea of having founded an institution that will not perish with your death, but will perpetuate the spirit and the feelings which called it into existence, in the minds and hearts of your children? This Home is the proudest of your enterprizes, the safest and most creditable of your investments. Of all your earthly possessions and treasures it is the only one of which you can say with certainty, "We shall leave it as a patrimony to our children." You cannot say this of the houses which you inhabit, and which you have not inherited from your ancestors. But the foundation, upon which our Home is erected, we have received as an inalienable and indestructible legacy from our fathers and shall bequeathe in like manner to our children. Upon this foundation—charity and love— our posterity will continue to raise superstructures more grand, more extensive still, for the benefit and salvation of mankind.

Of all the human efforts that excite our admiration, works of public utility and benefaction are the most salutary and precious. Every single act of charity bestowed upon an individual adorns the heart that prompted it, as every single virtue is an ornament to its possessor. But as a single virtue does not suffice, to conquer the evil propensities of our nature, so is an isolated alms inadequate to relieve general want, to alleviate general distress. All we know of it with certainty, is the generous emotion which thrills our heart in its bestowal; but we have no guarantee that the seed thus sown may not fall upon a barren soil. In depositing, however, our offerings of benevolence upon the altar of institutions designed for public benefaction, we can witness with our own eyes the fire, which descends from heaven, to consume the sacrifice.

The sight of the needy and the distressed causes your tender heart to ache; you bestow your gift, in order to soothe at once their pain and yours. But may not, in the very next hour, a similar spectacle of woe inflict a still deeper pain upon your heart, whilst you have not the power to soothe it? Now the public institution, sustained by general co-operation, affords you a guarantee of its permanent ability. Philanthropic corporations are established for specific purposes. The means entrusted to their hands must be employed in the furtherance of distinctly expressed ends, and cannot be diverted from their legitimate objects. The aggregate contributions of individuals become a consolidated fund, which forms the common property of the community. Private charity redounds to the credit of the individual, but public charitable institutions reflect honor upon the community and the nation.

And is any one bold enough to say, I am a member of this community, but a stranger to its noble efforts in the field of charity? I will have nor share, nor portion in the good and excellent works that are fostered on its bosom? Dare any one say, I belong to the nation, but I do not practice those virtues which constitute my nation's honor and greatness? As well may you say, I am a man, but am not affected by anything appertaining to humanity!

That charity is a distinguishing characteristic of our people, has so frequently been made the theme of charity orations, that I fear the re-statement of this proposition will be considered trite and threadbare. Yet a truth, however old, loses nothing of its force by repetition, more especially if it is strengthened by recent stubborn facts. I shall not, therefore, on this occasion, refer to the maxims of love and laws of charity taught and enjoined by the Inspired Volume, which constitutes the fountain of our faith and the standard of our actions; I shall not tire you with quotations from our national literature, dogmatical and ethical, in which the principles of universal benevolence are insisted upon as the indispensable criteria of a righteous life; nor shall I open the book of history to cull from the experience of past centuries such incidents as might strikingly illustrate the practical working of these principles and doctrines. Recent events are sufficient to corroborate our proposition.

Not many months ago the whole civilized world was startled by the intelligence, that the most shocking outrages had been committed in Syria. Fired by religious fanaticism, the Mohammedan Druses attacked their Christian fellow-subjects, and dealt out death and destruction among their defenceless victims. In their unholy and savage zeal they vowed to exterminate the "infidels" from the face of the land. Nor age, nor sex was spared. Thousands were cruelly massacred, whilst the remaining thousands sought their safety in flight, and were thus exposed to utter destitution, the horrors of starvation, and the cruel tortures that awaited them at the hands of their fierce enemies.

The pitiful cries of these wretched people had no sooner reached the shores of Europe, when sovereigns and statesmen and imperial legislatures were moving, to succor and protect their brothers-in-faith against the inflamed passions of the fanatic sons of the desert. But sovereigns and statesmen and imperial legislatures are swayed by political considerations, and accustomed to move within the circumscribed sphere of diplomatic prudence. From their exalted station they are wont to look only upon entire provinces and lands and peoples, whilst the distresses of individuals, or even the calamities of communities, rarely move their hearts to active intercession. The sufferers in Syria stood in need of immediate help. The voice of humanity, which is the voice of God, pleaded in their behalf. And it so happened that the first man who rightly and opportunely published to the world an interpretation of this voice—was a Jew. He is one of Israel's noblest sons, and has devoted, for the last quarter of a century, his time, his means and his energies to the amelioration of the condition of his oppressed and persecuted brethren in various countries and climes. Having so frequently listened to the groanings of his own co-religionists, his philanthropic heart instinctively warmed for the suffering strangers, and impelled him to prompt action. But his communication to the London Times, as simple in its style as sublime in its object, will speak for itself:

" *To the Editor of the Times:*

" SIR—I have noticed with the deepest sympathy, the statement made last evening in the House of Lords, that, owing to the recent outbreak in Syria, there are 20,000 of the Christian inhabitants, women and children, wandering over its mountains, exposed to the utmost peril. Being intimately acquainted with the nature of that country and the condition of its people, I appreciate, I am sorry to say, but too painfully, the vast amount of misery that must have been endured and is still prevalent.

" I believe that private benevolence may do something towards the alleviation of the distresses of the unhappy multitude now defenceless, homeless and destitute.

" I well know, from experience, the philanthropy of my fellow-countrymen, and I venture to think that the public would gladly and without delay contribute to the raising of a fund to be applied as circumstances may require, and under judicious management, for the relief of these unfortunate objects of persecution.

"I would suggest, therefore, that a small, active and influential committee be at once formed, with the view of raising subscriptions, and of placing themselves in communication with the British Consular authorities throughout Syria, so that assistance may be rendered by the remittance of money and the transmission of necessary supplies ; and I take the liberty of enclosing my check for £200, towards the proposed fund.

" * * * I have the honor to be, sir, yours faithfully,

"MOSES MONTEFIORE."

"East Cliff Lodge, Ramsgate,
July 10th, 1860.

But this is not an isolated instance. Simultaneously with this communication there appeared a letter of the same import, written by another eminent Jew, and published in the *Siecle*, of Paris. It was from the pen of the eloquent advocate and liberal statesman, whose voice at one time was potent in the councils of France, and who ranks among the first barristers of the Empire. After portraying the wretched condition of the sufferers, Mons. Cremieux thus proceeds:

"French Israelites! let us be the first to come to the help of our Christian brethren; let us not wait for the results of diplomacy, always so slow, which will regulate the future. Let us come to the help of these unfortunates. Let there, this very day, a large subscription be opened at Paris, and to-morrow an Israelitish committee be organized.

"Let us not lose one day, not one hour. Let the signal for a vast succor proceed from the midst of a Jewish body, formed in the capital of civilization. This signal will meet with a response from our brethren in England, Germany, Belgium, Holland, and all Europe, both in the countries which acknowledge them as citizens, and in those which still withhold from them this noble title.

"You, also, Jews of America, where liberty of worship marches triumphantly ; you, also, w'll come to the help of the Catholics in Asia, so cruelly oppressed by superstition. Let all of us bring our contribution to this holy work—the opulent Jew his large offering, the poor Jew his little mite.

"But a still grander idea may be expected to issue from this burst of devotion. Who knows ? God, who governs all things, has perhaps permitted this awful catastrophe, in order to afford the followers of all religions a solemn opportunity to assist each other to defend themselves against those furious animosities, daughters of superstition and barbarism. A permanent committee in every country, carefully watching all attacks made on the liberty of conscience, a general fund for the support of the victims of fanaticism without distinction of creed—this is the establishment which must be founded and sustained. Yes, the evils which at this moment innocent victims undergo, will awaken the sympathies of all. They will fructify the thought of protecting the future against the return of the scourge, which our age repels with horror—*religious persecution.*"

These efforts of two Jewish laymen were fully endorsed and actively supported by eminent ecclesiastical authorities. The Chief Rabbi of Great Britain, the highly esteemed and learned Dr. N. M. Adler, deemed the occasion of sufficient importance to issue a pastoral letter to his flock, in which the following passage occurs :

" I need not remind you that our holy religion, whose basis is the commandment, to love our neighbor as ourselves, urges upon us the duty of dispensing our charity without distinction of faith, sect or class—it enjoins upon us emphatically to deal out bread to the hungry, to console the afflicted, to cover the naked, and not to hide ourselves from those who are bone of our bone, and flesh of our flesh. However divided and separated we may be by seas mountains, languages and creeds, still we are descended from the same Father, the same God has created us, we belong to the same undivided, original family."

A letter from Bordeaux, in the London *Times*, announces that the Grand Rabbi of that city, together with the members of the Consistory, presented themselves at the Archbishop's Palace, and handed to Cardinal Donnet the produce of a collection made by their co-religionists in favor of the Christians in Syria.

Nay, more than this. A number of boys belonging

to the sorely-oppressed congregation of Rome, made a collection among themselves, and transmitted the same to Mr. Cremieux, to be applied to the relief of the Syrian Christians. Mr. Cremieux acknowledges the receipt of this contribution and the accompanying appropriate letter, under date of September 5, 1860, in the following beautiful words:

"*My Dear Children :*

"Your pious gift and the touching letter accompanying it are at hand. Foster within you these good and noble feelings, the seeds of which are planted in your juvenile hearts. There is nothing more pleasing to God than sympathy with the unfortunate. There is not a more sacred command than this : "Thou shalt love thy neighbor as thyself." And in the century in which we live, my dear children, the neighbor, whom we are commanded to love, is the man who suffers, no matter what faith he may profess or in what religion he may have been born. The God, whom we worship, wills, that we succor the distressed." * * *

Now, if we bear in mind that these strenuous charitable efforts were made by Jews in behalf of those very Christians, who in the year 1840 had inflicted the cruelest persecutions which fanaticism could devise, upon the Jewish inhabitants of Damascus, we are justified in asserting if stern facts and undeniable deeds prove anything—that charity, in its amplest sense, is a distinguishing characteristic of our people, inculcated by our religion, taught in our schools and Synagogues, living in our hearts, and influencing our conduct.

For ourselves there would be no need of recapitulating and emphasizing these occurrences, further than advert to them as bright examples worthy of our emulation. We know that they are the natural out-pourings of deeply-rooted and fondly-cherished sentiments, which we hold in common with Israelites all over the globe. But the charge of unfeeling exclusiveness and sectarian narrow-mindedness (to use the mildest terms) is so frequently dinned into our ears and repeated *ad nauseam usque*, by prejudiced journalists, writers of fiction, and even authors of serious literature, that an occasional refutation of these scurrilous skeptics—not only ceases to be a violation of the rules of modesty, but is rendered necessary by the peculiarity of our position. The Scriptural proverb, " Let another man praise thee, and not thy own mouth ; a stranger, and not thy own lips," can only have reference to vain-glorious boastings, or over-weening claims to fancied or real superiority over others; but if our individual or national character be aspersed, then a vindication of our honor and dignity by an appeal to truth, is in consonance alike with common sense and the most rigid notions of propriety and morality.

For ourselves, we need not cast our eyes beyond the boundaries of our city, in order to point to instances of practical Jewish charity, emanating from individuals or communities. The name of Judah Touro, of blessed memory, is a host in itself, whilst our noble institution, the creation of our united efforts, bears testimony to the fact that we do not hide ourselves from the cry of distress. The celebration of our anniversary should, therefore, enlist our liveliest interest and enthusiasm. To rejoice in the happiness of others is the purest and most heavenly joy which the human heart is capable of indulging. It is the strongest test of genuine love. Hence it is that to be instrumental in founding the happiness of those, who otherwise might remain a prey to misery and wretchedness, is to man a source of unalloyed gratification. Can we this day, after five years' experience, contemplate with indifference the amount of good effected by our Home ? Is it nothing to us, to have aided in drying the tear of the widow—in providing for the wants of the orphan—in giving a home to the homeless? Is it nothing to us, to have aided in neutralizing the fearful effects of poverty leagued with sickness, by removing at least the care and want from decrepid age, and substituting therefor the smiles of ease and plenty? Is it nothing to us, to have adopted the fatherless, and to superintend their physical well-being, and their moral and religious training? Have we not good reason to rejoice in the happy results which, under Providence, our young institution has been instrumental in producing?

Wealth and poverty—affluence and want—prosperity and adversity, are no idle terms in the dictionary of life. They designate an actual state of things. How many of our fellow-beings are subjected to unspeakable privations and cares, while others are enjoying comfort and ease, and others again reveling in the luxuries and superfluities of the world. The social economy is mysterious in its arrangements. Yet the Bible teaches, "And God saw all that he had made, and behold, it was very good." This necessary dependence, then, of one class of society on the other, may be turned, and does, in fact, redound to our good. For when may man feel happier and more conscious of his worth than in the act of relieving the burden of his neighbor? The divine spark of love is kindled in his bosom, and love begets charity, and charity begets happiness. In parting, therefore, with a slight portion of that substance of which we are but temporary stewards, in aid of individuals or the support of institutions of public benefaction, we practically acknowledge the benefits which our all-kind Father has bestowed upon us, and feel exalted in the reflection that he has favored us to be the distributors of his bounty.

But whilst indulging the pleasing emotions, which our anniversary must needs awaken in our hearts—

whilst congratulating ourselves upon the happy results thus far achieved through the agency of our Home, let us not relax in our efforts to establish our institution upon a still more solid and permanent basis. So long as the existence of our noble charity is likely to be affected by the vicissitudes of the times and the reverses of individual fortunes—so long as its income is likely to be regulated by the "profit and loss" of the community—so long as its destiny is bound up with the ever-shifting successes and failures of commercial enterprize—so long we cannot say that it will be equal to all emergencies, or certain of perpetuity. It is only then, when a permanent fund shall have been secured sufficiently large to cover, by its revenue, the greater portion of our expenditure, that we can say, Our Home is protected against every storm, and able to dispense its benefits, as heretofore, without stint and without intermission. The fund thus far accumulated is too small to insure the end proposed, and looks for its gradual increase to our Anniversary gatherings. Shall it be said that the prevailing crisis, harrassing and distressing though it may be, should deter us, on this occasion, from acting in the spirit of our accustomed liberality? The more keenly we may feel the prostration of our own hopes, the more strongly should we be impressed with our duty, not to deceive the hopes of those whom Providence has placed in our charge, and who await protection and maintenance at our hands.

Fathers and mothers! you, around whose bosoms the tender chords of parental affection—those endearing bonds of nature's workmanship—are lovingly entwined, think, O think, if your own children (which our heavenly Father avert) were to be left by the inscrutable designs of Providence in the cold and chilly orphanage of life—left to suffer the hunger, and the want, and the destitution, which, no doubt, many of you in your benevolent missions have painfully witnessed—left to the fortuitous mercy of the world: would not your souls glow with gratitude in the realms of eternity towards the good and charitable, who would stretch forth their hands and protect and guide your offspring? How know you, that among the little band of our adopted children there are not some, whose infancy gave promise of as bright a destiny as is smiling on yours? How know you, in the uncertainty of all human things, what may be the lot of the babes you love?

Husbands, you, whose heart rejoices in the affection of a beloved and loving wife—who cherish her with a devotion that is ever bent upon strewing the roses of comfort and peace around her path, upon shielding her tender nature against the rude storms of adversity—who feel happy in the thought of being near her, to share her joy, to chase away her sorrow, and to enable her to perform the duties of life with a blissful and contented serenity—would you not bless the hand extended to her in the dread hour of bereavement and trial? Would you not invoke a benediction upon the abode where, in her declining years, her wants would be supplied, and the pangs of her loneliness be soothed by the sympathy of kind and benevolent hearts?

Young men! you, who have grown up in the lap of abundance—whose infancy and childhood were the constant objects of a father's kind solicitude, of a mother's tender care and watchfulness—whose wishes required no talisman but the expression—who enjoyed the protection and guidance of affectionate parents to warn you against vice and inure you to virtue—do not your souls glow with sympathy for those of your fellow-beings, who were born like yourselves, with muscles, and nerves,

10

and hearts, and every capacity for suffering, but are bereft of their natural protectors?

Be ready then, to-day, to testify by your generous donations the sincerity of your compassion and benevolent sentiments. It is a debt of gratitude which all of you owe to the Dispenser of all good. Give extension and permanency—and you can do it—to our noble institution. Let the generosity of your own natures supply what may be defective in my appeal. Cramp not the benevolent expansion of your hearts. Paralyze not the sublime impulses of your nature. Weigh not on the finger of cold and niggard calculation the contributions you are to offer. Let the amount to be realized warrant us in increasing our permanent fund, and thus afford an additional guarantee to the stability and perpetuity of our Home.

XIII.

ADDRESS

Delivered at the

FUNERAL OF JUDAH TOURO,

AT NEW ORLEANS, LA.

Friday, January 20th, 1854.

A GOOD man has departed; a righteous Israelite has been gathered to his fathers. Judah Touro is no more. His soul has returned to God; his earthly remains are about to be borne to the silent tomb. He reached the advanced age of 78 years and 7 months, having been a resident of this city for 52 years.

The death of the good and benevolent never fails to strike a sympathetic chord in the hearts of the survivors. Regret and sorrow at their loss become manifest. And these feelings are the more general, the more deep, the more earnest—the wider the sphere in which this goodness was displayed, the broader the scale on which this benevolence was practised. Among the crowd of mourners assembled around this coffin, there is none who is related to the deceased by ties of consanguinity. Yet, may I venture to assert, that many a heart throbs with genuine grief, that many an eye drops a genuine tear, as if lamenting the death of a brother, the loss of a father.

What is it, that has won for our departed friend the hearts of his fellow-citizens? What is it, that has gained him the love and esteem of all who knew him? What is it, that has made his name shed a lustre on our city, and caused it to be pronounced in the most distant sections of our country, with an affectionate reverence? It is not the brilliancy of his mind—for he had no pretensions to learning or scholarship; it is not his political influence—for he loved retirement; it is not the splendor of his establishment—for he was notorious for the simplicity of his habits; nor is it even his wealth—for there are many, who possess a vastly larger amount of earthly substance, whose names, nevertheless, do not emerge from obscurity, nor command the love and esteem of their contemporaries. Judah Touro is renowned and respected for his broad philanthropy, for his unprejudiced charity. His qualities emanated directly from the heart, and could not fail to win the heart. He was public-spirited without parade; he delighted in doing good, without ostentation; his greatest weakness was his antipathy to see his name published to the world; the consciousness of having done a good action was to him sufficient reward.

I shall not, therefore, on this occasion, offend his memory, by attempting to give a specific account of the extent of his liberality. Nor is it within my power to do so. The hundreds and the thousands which he devoted to patriotic objects, or to the relief of general distress, may be partially known—but who can tell us the amount of individual suffering, which his timely aid alleviated? Who has registered the names of distressed widows, of forlorn orphans, of destitute strangers, that were the recipients of his bounty? However lonely he may have felt in the declining years of his pilgrimage on earth, the deeds of benevolence, the friendly acts of kindness which he had noiselessly performed, must have clustered round his heart like guardian angels, shedding a light on his path, and pointing forward to a bright future.

The philanthropy of the deceased knew no distinction of creed or nationality. He did not confine his charity to the pale of his own religion. He considered Jew and Gentile to have an equal claim on him. Wherever he deemed his assistance well applied, he was ready to render it. Individuals and corporations can bear testimony to this beautiful trait in his character. In his life and actions were exemplified the words of the prophet, " Have we not all one Father? has not one God created us? why then should we be treacherous one against the other?"

But whilst rendering justice to his high virtues as a man, whilst admiring his unimpeachable integrity, his general benevolence, his unstinted charity, the constancy of his attachment to his friends, and the uniform kindness to his servants—we cannot pass by in silence his noble qualities as a citizen. Among the ranks of the brave patriots who, in 1814 and 1815 defended our city against foreign invasion, Judah Touro was to be found. Nor did he escape unharmed. The effects of the fatal ball that struck him, clung to him for the remainder of his life. Though conservative in his views, he has contributed materially to the improvement of the city, by ornamenting our principal streets with some of the finest mercantile edifices, which reflect credit on this Southern emporium of commerce. And truly may we apply to him the words of Solomon, " By the blessing of the righteous the city is exalted."

Within this city, too, he has left a lasting monument to his munificence and his religious fervor. A descendant of Abraham, a firm believer in the One God, who has created heaven and earth, who has revealed his word from amidst the thunders of Sinai—he has founded and endowed a Synagogue, in which the time-hallowed worship of Israel is performed, in which the Law is read and the Hymns of David are chaunted in their original tongue. And thus the evening of his life was cheered up by the delight and solace which he derived from a regular attendance at that place of worship, and the solemn communion with his Maker.

And this good man has passed away. No more shall we look on his venerable form; no more shall we receive the hearty grasp of his hand. But his name will not be forgotten, his memory will be blessed by generations to come. He bore with fortitude the ills of his decline, and prepared himself for the approaching end. And when at last his senses were veiled by the shadows of death, and all earthly objects had faded from his view—then could be plainly discerned, from his occasional low murmurings, the repeated prayerful ejaculations, "Oh God," "Holy Father!"—indicating his firm trust in God, his hope in a blissful immortality.

XIV.

ADDRESS

Delivered at the

FUNERAL OF JUDAH TOURO,

AT NEWPORT, R. I.

Tuesday, June 7th, 1854.

FULL seventy-nine years have elapsed—two generations have since passed away—when, within the precincts of this town, Judah Touro was ushered into life. Like his ancestor Jacob, he took the pilgrim-staff in hand—from the North he travelled to the then distant South. Like the patriarch, the Lord was with him and prospered his ways; like the patriarch, it was his last injunction, " When I shall sleep with my fathers, then carry me away and bury me in their burying-place." To-day, therefore, we are gathered round the bier of the departed, and are about to conduct his earthly remains to their final resting-place, that they may sleep side by side with the ashes of long departed kindred.

The life of Judah Touro is marked by none of those brilliant achievements, by none of those dazzlingly striking incidents, which are generally considered to constitute human greatness. His word never marshalled into battle array, and led to victory the hosts of his countrymen; his voice resounded not in the halls of legislation, nor had he the gift, "the applause of listening Senates to command." But in all that is truly honorable, and generous, and noble, he was foremost among the foremost. His heart was instinct with that true benevolence, which forces the tear of sympathy into the eye, and opens the hand to succor and to relieve. A sublime goodness characterized his actions, an exalted virtue adorned his life. The warm impulses of a generous soul gushed forth from nature's purest fountain.

His charity, like his friendship, knew of neither sectional nor sectarian boundaries. The catholicity of the one was equalled by the constancy of the other. Modest and unpretending, meek and humble, even to a fault, he delighted in going good in secret, and felt happy in the consciousness of being the unknown cause of the happiness of others.

And to these virtues and principles he remained true to the end of his days. Years will roll on—another generation will succeed us—many a name, now shining in the meridian of its glory, will be forgotten ; yet the name and memory of Judah Touro will ever live in the hearts of posterity. Through the length and breadth of this country, the name of this philanthropist will ever be coupled with the beautiful words of Scripture, " The memory of the just will be for a blessing."

Yes, my friends, the memory of the deceased will ever be blessed. Whether we consider his character as a man, as a citizen, or as an Israelite, it equally claims our admiration, our affectionate regard. Through his munificient bequests, so liberally and so judiciously distributed, he has erected to himself numerous monuments, more durable than moulded bronze or chiselled marble, which the gratitude of others may raise. The religious and educational seminaries, the asylums for the poor and suffering—which he has either established or endowed—

for the ennobling of the heart, the improvement of the mind, and the alleviation of distress, are bright evidences of the deep interest he felt for all that tends to ameliorate the moral and physical condition of man. The Touro Infirmary, the Touro Almshouse, the Synagogue, founded by the deceased in that Southern metropolis, which had been his constant residence for more than half a century; the Touro Tablets, which will decorate the walls of many a hospital, asylum, school and sacred place of worship throughout this country, will ever bear witness to those heavenly feelings of benevolence and philanthropy, which animated his good and pious soul.

"The fruit of the just is a tree of life." Such a tree of life, affording shade and shelter to many a weary pilgrim, has been planted by the deceased.

Are we, then, met to grieve at his death? Not, certainly, for the sake of the departed. He had passed the ordinary goal; he had fulfilled his great mission and was waiting for his recall. Sensible of the approach of his end, convinced of a happy immortality, death was to him the commencement of a higher life—an admission to the benign presence of his Father, who is also our Father—of his God, who is also our God.

Shall we mourn the loss we have sustained? Time mellows and corrects our feelings. The predominant emotion of my bosom is, profound gratitude to heaven for giving us such a man, and sparing him so long. I lose my regret that he is dead, in my deep joy, that he has lived. And this I believe to be the general sentiment of his brethren and friends, of the trustees and recipients of his bounty. The priceless value of such a man is thus best appreciated. In the contemplation of his life we should become profoundly and solemnly impressed with a conviction of the infinite importance, which may be given to the life of man on earth by a beautiful and conscientious devotion, of all the means at command, to the nurture and development of the soul's highest faculties, to the culture and manifestation of the soul's purest affections.

This occasion, then, is not one of exclusive mourning, for the sake of either the dead or the living, but rather one for the expression of fervent gratitude for the precious example of such a life and death, for the lessons of true wisdom it is designed to teach, and for the devout and lofty aspirations, which it should excite. In this spirit let it be improved by us; in this spirit let us raise our hearts in prayer to our Creator and heavenly Protector.

XV.

ADDRESS

Delivered at the Dedication of the

TOMB OF THE HOWARD ASSOCIATION

OF NEW ORLEANS,

AND THE TRANSFER OF THE REMAINS OF ITS PRESIDENT

VICTOR BOULLEMET,

Sunday, April 15th, 1860.

YOU are assembled here, to perform a solemn ceremony, a self-imposed duty. You are about to remove from their temporary vault the cherished remains of a co-laborer in your work of charity and benevolence, and deposit them in the newly-erected tomb, which bears the name of the immortal philanthropist, whose sublime example you have chosen for your guide. The act, in which you are engaged, is no vain ovation to the living, but a sincere tribute of respect to the memory of departed worth. It is an illustration of the fact, that associations like yours, formed for purposes of pure benevolence, serve to keep alive and active the kindly sensibilities of the heart, by inducing an observance of the tender and humane duties which ennoble our nature.

Nearly four years have elapsed, since we were engaged in solemnizing the sad funeral rites on the mortal remains of Virgil Boullemet, your late lamented president. Cut off, as he was, in the prime of life, by a disease which he contracted in the active paths of his humane exertions, his death was one of those mysterious and dark dispensations of that Providence " whose ways are not as man's ways"—a dispensation which, bringing home to the most careless, the sense of the frail tenure of life, awes the mind into stillness and solemnity. But severely as the blow must have been felt by the dearer friends of his own family, the sorrow of others for the loss of a virtuous man, whose life had been ardently devoted to the service of humanity, to the amelioration of the condition of the sick and the needy, has in it little of bitterness. It is sad, and solmen, and calm, and durable.

The deceased requires no studied eulogy, no ostentatious panegyric at my hands. You, his fellow-laborers, who have been both witnesses and sharers of his labors of love, will coincide with me, when I say that his eulogy is written in the hearts of thousands yet living, to whom he proved, under Providence, " an angel of mercy that bore healing on his wings," whilst thousands, whose pains he was instrumental in soothing, but whose lives he was unable to save, pronounced with their last breaths the most effective panegyric before the very throne of the Eternal.

You are surrounded by the emblems of death. Within these vaults sleep many of those, who were dear to you in life, with whom you exchanged a friendly grasp, whom you warmly pressed to your bosom. The light of their eyes once beaming intelligence and love, is quenched; their hearts have ceased to beat; their noble forms, once instinct with manly vigor or melting beauty, have mouldered to dust. But above us there shineth forth the bright orb of day, and the blue arch of heaven is stretched out in immeasurable expanse, suggesting the idea of infinitude; of eternity. And whilst daily experience teaches us that sad lesson, that "in the midst of life we are in death," the voice of nature, which is also the voice

God, strikes the consoling conviction into our hearts, that from the midst of death we look forward to life eternal, to immortality.

> "The soul, secured in her existence, smiles
> At the drawn dagger, and defies its point;
> The stars shall fade away, the sun himself
> Grow dim with age, and nature sink in years,
> But thou shalt flourish in immortal youth,
> Unhurt amidst the war of elements,
> The wreck of matter, and the crash of worlds."

To erect tombs, where the temple of clay once tenanted by the immortal foul, is to be enshrined, is a noble custom. It is in consonance with the deepest feelings of human nature. These tombs become sacred shrines, where not only the *names* of the departed are snatched from oblivion, but where their virtues and generous deeds are remembered for good. Many a weary pilgrim, whose steps will be arrested on passing this spot, and reading the noble name engrossed upon this tomb, will speak with the poet:

> "Peace to the good man's memory,—let it grow
> Greener with years, and blossom thro' the flight of ages;
> Let the light
> Stream on his deeds of love, that shunned the sight
> Of all but Heaven, and in the book of fame
> The glorious record of his virtues write,
> And hold it up to men, and bid them claim
> A palm like his, and catch from him the hallowed flame."

XVI.

ADDRESS
Delivered at the
FUNERAL OF JOSEPH FATMAN,
AT NEW YORK,
Sunday, October 10th 1869.

A GOOD MAN has departed; a righteous Israelite has been gathered to his fathers. Joseph Fatman is no more. His soul has returned to God; his earthly remains are about to be borne to the silent tomb.

How solemn are the reflections that arise in our minds, in performing the last sad office of love, which the living may minister to the dead, how serious the lesson thus afforded! The feeling of our nothingness, of our frailty, of the precarious tenure of life, and the certainty of death, strikes our soul with overpowering conviction; and prayerfully we look up to him, who is the source of eternal life, upon whom we are dependent, and in whom we trust in life and in death. But amidst these solemn emotions, our memory involuntarily reverts to the lamented departed, and we can scarcely realize the fact, that he has been called away from his work on earth " to that eternal bourne from whence no traveller returns."

" Man is but a pilgrim here below." Such is the language of Holy Scripture, such the expression that so frequently greets our ear, when the career of an earthly pilgrimage is closed in death. This aphorism is no figure of speech, but an incontrovertible truth, a stern reality. We may ignore it amidst the struggling activities and diversified pursuits of life; we may strive and work, labor and toil, plant and build, as if the earth were our eternal home, yet the hour will come, sooner or later, that will call us from our task, and force us to relinquish our post. In that hour, when our account with earth is settled, the value of our life is not measured by our worldly success and possessions, but by our exertions for the good of others, for the amelioration of the suffering, and the promotion of the welfare and happiness of our fellow-mortals.

Measured by this standard, the life of the deceased assumes a high value. Engaged in commercial pursuits, which but too often cramp the kindlier impulses of human nature, he achieved success without sacrificing the good will and kindly regards of his neighbors, while his heart remained instinct with that true benevolence which prompts the active deed. If any evidence of the genuine worth of the private and public virtues of our departed friend were needed, it is amply furnished by this large gathering of mourning friends, who, in his demise, deplore the loss of a good, honorable man, of a zealous laborer in the cause of charity. The goodness of his soul was not confined to the narrow sphere of home, but was cheerfully exerted for the benefit of his fellow-mortals at large. The noble qualities of mind and heart, with which God had blessed him, were not suffered to congeal by selfishness, but warmed into life and deeds of benevolence and love. On the memorial-tablets of those sacred institutions of humanity, that are flourishing in our midst, the name of Joseph Fatman will ever occupy an honorable place. The Mount Sinai Hospital, and the Hebrew

Orphan Asylum have been principally benefited, not only by his munificent contributions, but by his personal attention and labors; and many an hour he snatched from the enjoyments of home and business pursuits, to promote the welfare of those institutions. And thus cut off in the maturity of manhood, the deceased has not lived in vain. And although the highest term of human age was not vouchsafed to him—although he was not spared to enjoy a season of rest, of recreation, of undisturbed enjoyment of life's blessings in life's tranquil evening hours, yet welcome and promising must be to him the dawn of eternal life, since his earthly career closed upon a useful activity, and the palm of approbation and love of all who knew him, will decorate his peaceful grave.

But whilst deeply deploring the loss which our community has sustained in the death of so good and charitable a man, I shrink from intruding upon the sacred privacy of grief, which this bereavement has inflicted upon the immediate family of the lamented deceased. Yet, can we forbear expressing our sympathy for, and mingling our tears with the tears of the sorrow-stricken widow, who has lost the companion of her youth, the protector and solace of her declining age? Can we forbear feeling a sympathy for, and mingling our tears with the tears of the sorrowing children, who mourn the loss of an affectionate and devoted father? On these profoundly solemn occasions, when the perishableness of our earthly existence strikes our hearts with irresistible force, when our horizon is shrouded in darkness and gloom, we look up to God, and derive comfort and courage from our faith in his eternal goodness and mercy. The conviction that our soul is immortal, the hope that we shall one day be reunited with those who were dear to us on earth, must exercise a soothing influence on our grief, and cause the mourner to submit with resignation to the will of Providence. On the earthly form of the departed we cast a last, loving, lingering look, but his spirit has returned to his God, into the realm of eternal life and bliss; the seeds of love and of virtue, which he has sown in the hearts of his children, will bear ennobling fruit and immortalize his name and his lineage, while his deeds of benevolence and charity, and his memory, will be for a blessing.

XVII.

OPENING PRAYER

Delivered at the Semi-Centennial Anniversary

OF THE

Hebrew Benevolent and Orphan Asylum Society

OF NEW YORK,

Thursday, April 11th, 1872.

ALMIGHTY GOD! Creator of heaven and earth! Father of all mankind!—With a deep sense of our dependence upon Thy loving kindness, we approach Thee on this festive and gratifying occasion, and bless Thy Holy Name. Thou art our Everlasting Shield and Heavenly Protector; " with Thee is the source of life;" from the fount of Thy revelation do we derive light; and by Thy infinite mercy are we sustained.

Allkind Father!—Love is the effulgence of Thy glory; love is the eternal pillar that supporteth the universe; the mysterious link that holds in unison worlds without end; the heavenly tie that binds Thy children to Thee, that unites and fraternizes the sons of man.

Omnipotent God! Thou commandest—and spheres spring into existence; Thou speakest—and life throbs through the pulses of creation. The eyes of all hopefully wait upon Thee; for Thou openest Thy hand and providest for all living beings, and Thy mercy extendeth over all Thy works. Blessed art Thou, O Lord, our God, who hast preserved us alive and sustained us in health, to participate in this jubilee of charity.

We thank Thee, O God, for the protection which Thou hast extended towards our Society. Small was its beginning, but its sphere has wonderfully increased in extent and in usefulness. Devoted originally to the incidental relief of the poor and needy, it has established a home for the homeless, where the tears of the orphan are dried, and helpless innocence finds comfort and protection. The tree, planted fifty years ago by the hand of charity in the soil of humanity, now affords a grateful shade to those who are sheltered under its branches.

Guide and strengthen us, O God, in the direction of our efforts to alleviate, in some degree, the distresses that are incident to human life. May Thy blessing rest upon the Asylum and upon all those that have found, and are yet destined to find shelter under its roof. May harmony, kindness and love link together all its children as members of one family—and virtue and piety be their portion of inheritance, their inalienable guides through life.

And we beseech Thee, O God, to bless the officers, patrons and members of the Society, and all those who have nobly contributed, and those who will hereafter contribute towards its support. May their generous zeal continue unabated, and warm hearts and liberal hands at all times be ready to aid in the prosecution of so sacred a cause. What greater happiness can there be for man, than to ameliorate the condition of his fellow-man, to render cheerful the otherwise gloomy lot of the widow and the fatherless! Reward, we pray Thee, the sacrifices made in behalf of the Hebrew Benevolent and Orphan Asylum Society in the plenitude of Thy grace!

This fiftieth anniversary of the institution must needs reminds us of the transitoriness of human life. Its found ers and many of its members have returned to their eternal home, to reap the reward of their good deeds done upon earth—and we bless their memory in this solemn hour. Grant, O God, that the living patrons, members and supporters, be long spared in health and prosperity to witness and enjoy the happy results attained by their sacrifices and well-directed charitable efforts.

Continue, O God, Thy heavenly protection over our beloved country. May it increase in renown, in prosperity and in virtue. May peace, harmony and obedience to law prevail among the people, and the various sections ever be closely united by the bonds of true patriotism and brotherly love.

Bless, O Father, all those here assembled. May the occasion not pass by without a salutary effect, but be conducive to the steady cultivation and development of the blissful feelings of benevolence and philanthropy in thought, in word, and in deed.

And may the grace of the Lord, our God, be upon us; and the work of our hand be firmly established upon us; yea, the work of our hand do Thou firmly establish it, whom we adore as our God and our Father for evermore. Amen.

www.ingramcontent.com/pod-product-compliance
Lightning Source LLC
Chambersburg PA
CBHW031444160426
43195CB00010BB/848